The New Economic Agenda

FINANCIAL

The New Economic Agenda

Edited by Mary Inglis and Sandra Kramer

FINDHORN PRESS

ISBN 0 905249 61 5

First published 1985
Copyright © individual contributors 1984

Set in 11/12 point Garamond by Findhorn Publications.
Book and cover design by Findhorn Foundation Design Group.
Printed and bound by John G. Eccles Printers Ltd., Inverness, Scotland.

Published by The Findhorn Press, The Park, Forres IV36 OTZ, Scotland.

The cover design for this book, which was also the logo for the conference
on 'The New Economic Agenda', suggests the need for positive spiritual,
cultural and material values in our current economic transformation. The
computer represents clean technology, available to all, while the bread and
fishes represent abundance for all. The fish and the pitcher of water sym-
bolise the merging of Piscean and Aquarian values.

Contents

5

P.7

**Something is astir in the land of economics.
The territory which has for so long been
'the dismal science' is showing signs that
it is about to undergo a
powerful transformation....**

Guy Dauncey

SOMETHING IS STIRRING - MONEY MATTERS

IN THE LAND OF THE HOME + THE BRAVE -

SOMETHING IS STIRRING - MONEY

IN THIS LAND OF KNOW FOR IT IS PERSUIT

LIFE - LIBERTY - HAPPINESS -

IS ABOUT A POWERFUL TRANSFORMATION

Foreword

Francois Duquesne

The following book is made up of talks given at a conference of the Findhorn Foundation in October 1984. Entitled 'The New Economic Agenda' its aim was to bring together practitioners from both the conventional and alternative fields of economics in order to share experiences and reflect on some of the trends that are shaping the emerging *Fin* economic landscape of the 80s and 90s.

By no means is this a complete statement. What is gathered here represents a variety of perspectives that bear upon the personal, local, national and global dimensions of a transformative approach to economics. Other initiatives such as the London-based Business Network (a forum for exploring the human factor in business) and The Other Economic Summit (a gathering of alternative economists that parallels the annual summit of the leaders of the ten largest western industrial states) have also begun to assess from their own vantage point the nature of the changes currently under way. From the onset this conference was designed to be a cooperative venture, as we sought to work with various groups and to elicit from speakers and participants alike their own unique contributions, being careful not to prejudge too quickly what does and does not belong to the new economic agenda.

The topics range from personal attitudes towards lack and prosperity to the changing role of work, from the creation of small community businesses and entrepreneurial networks to the political impact of the new economics, and finally include a first-hand and fascinating look at the economics of developing countries.

Remarkable in such a diverse group of people were the qualities of integrity, sincerity and dedication they all embodied in the pursuit of their goals and beliefs. It is certainly worth noting that many of the salient features that characterise the world of successful business as described by the authors of *In Search of Excellence* were also highly distinctive of this assembly: 'hands-on', 'value-driven', 'biased towards action', and above all an ethics of 'people matter most' and 'people come first'.

The conference itself sought to emphasise the theme of wholeness as an underpinning of the new edifice. Mornings were given over to lectures, afternoons to rest, recreation, workshops and small groups for the deepening of personal understanding, while the evenings were split between further presentations and musical events.

As the week evolved we began to realise how much had been gathered and shared, how many friendships and partnerships had been formed and how real wealth can be created through the process of community, the 'coming together' of hearts and minds. We hope that some of this excitement will be communicated to you through the following testimonies.

Part I

The New Economics:
Personal and Political

PART I

THE NEW POLITICALLY
BACKED FIN. 57'

PART II

TITE NEW PERSINAL TRANSFORMATION

9

Echo-nomics:
The Science of Come-Back

Lionel Fifield

Lionel Fifield is a chartered accountant and founder of the Brisbane Relaxation Centre which many recognise as the leading personal growth centre of Australia. A popular and dynamic lecturer on communication, human potential, prosperity consciousness and stress handling, he has the gift of bringing a light and humour-filled touch to these subjects.

How rare it is that people go to economics conferences for a good laugh! A good laugh does so much good; it takes people out of all their seriousness and their non-creative state of worry. When I work with business groups I sometimes suggest we take a moment or two to relax before we start, to let go of the stress of life and enter a state of peace and creativity. People usually start heading for the door at that point. It is as if I were trying to take away their right arm. To let go of stress after so many years is a very frightening thing to do. But, to me, the next economy deals very much with *quality* of life—especially in what we call the well-to-do nations, where so many people are killing themselves unnecessarily instead of focusing in and enjoying themselves.

In the next economy people will move into being much more part of all that is, rather than thinking it's a question of getting out there and knocking the hell out of everything to win. We will get to a state of 'win-win' instead of 'win-lose'. I call this economy 'echo-nomics', the science of come-back, or 'as you sow so you reap'. It's the law of karma, of cause and effect; 'givers gain, takers lose'; 'those who live by the sword, die by the sword'; 'as we judge, so we are judged'. In other words, it means taking responsibility for ourselves and our thinking, and realising the importance of our attitudes, perceptions and the way we treat other people. It means understanding that each individual is a powerful beacon and magnet, and that whatever we do or think is affecting ourselves and everybody around us.

In the past we have tended to get very serious about being objective and analysing the state of the world. Rather than analysing too seriously I think we have to move in. Many physicists are now saying that they cannot be separate from what they study. The same is true with economists. They can't be separate from the economy of their own lives and what is around them. One of the finest definitions I have heard of a prophet is not a person who sits and tells other people how they are going to be in 20 years time but someone who basically *demonstrates* to people how things will be in 20 years time. This fits in with what Albert Schweitzer said about there being only three ways in which it is possible positively to change people: the first is by example, the second is by example and—yes, you've got it—the third is by example.

Here we are then, beginning to realise we can be masters instead of victims. It is fascinating how money has become a master in our society. We have lost control over it. When you suggest to people that they could become masters of this energy, they laugh. But we have the choice of taking control, because that is the dominion we have over these things, or of deciding to be the servants of money, which is the way of thinking we have accepted up to now. Maybe it's not by chance that there's a credit card called Mastercard!

I have seen groups of business people get together to discuss a new project and they become really excited about it until someone says, "Of course, there is one problem—money." Suddenly all these people who are in control of huge funds as individuals and professionals sink back into their chairs. It is very rare that someone is prepared to be the first to stand up and say, "Hey, I'm going to start this." What normally happens is that the saviour of the group stands up and mentions that the government are giving subsidies to people like them, and an overwhelming air of wonder goes around the whole group; they don't have to give anything themselves. They go sailing off, having delegated one of their number to go for the money. But how sad that is! They have given up and handed the responsibility to someone else.

When I first arrived in Australia some years ago, an Englishman came up to me and said: "You'll find these Australians a very unusual bunch. If your car breaks down, you can stand at the side of the road and wave for help and people will wave back and drive right on. The thing to do, even if your car is a big one and it's facing uphill, is to get behind it and start pushing, even though it seems an impossible task.

Aussies will immediately appear from everywhere to help push you wherever you want to go." A few years after that I began to realise that the world we live in is very similar. If we stop seeing what makes a project impossible and stop looking for the easy, manipulative ways out, and decide instead to go ahead with something because it feels good and we know it is right to do, it's as if the whole universe is full of Aussies: they're behind you and somehow or other all that you need comes together. That, of course, was the basis the Findhorn Foundation was built on. When I was an accountant and first came here I thought what a peculiar but exciting place it was. Nothing I had been taught when I studied accountancy was happening here. But there was something far more dynamic taking place. I hadn't learnt then about the energy of money or the power of thought.

The new economy involves a very wide process of change. Sometimes in seminars with business groups I can sense people sitting there thinking, "I'm here, but don't think you can change me." It makes me so sad, because what they are really saying is, "I don't want to find me." They don't realise that within them is a being of beauty, love and power, and that everything they are going through will help them move into what is most appropriate for them. Stress is costing them and our society a fortune, in whatever way you want to measure a fortune. Much of the future economy will be based on people's ability to relax and listen, to move into their potential. When we can hear ourselves, we can hear other people—the employers and employees and unemployed, the 'with-it' nations and those without. We can start communicating effectively, rather than pinning on each other ideas we learnt years ago which are no longer appropriate. Let us not forget that the greatest cause of stress is fear of change. As we are able to accommodate that change, so can we move rapidly ahead.

When I do workshops I am amazed at how many people even in 'good' jobs lack self-esteem. In the next economy, education in companies and universities will help us feel better about ourselves. Then we will feel better about everything we do. Echo-nomics is how we attract what we feel—so if we feel bad about ourselves, then the world, the firm, the employer, the employees also seem bad. Instead, we can open up and discover the absolute marvel we dream of.

When I first began to explore some of these so-called laws of echo-nomics, I began to notice how some people were constantly running into problems, even though they had good ideas. I couldn't understand why some people were consistently successful while others were consistently 'failures'. And I noticed that other people who were successful with their money were unsuccessful in other aspects of their lives. I began to see how many people, whatever their outer expression, were thinking lack and were fearing not being able to do. They were reaching out for others to subsidise them all the time instead of knowing they had the power to carry out their own visions.

As I began to see this more clearly, it occurred to me to start giving courses on prosperity. As a start I thought I would see what the prosperity teachers of this world charge for their courses. It was fascinating to discover that many of them were charging $500 or $1000 for a weekend. They obviously didn't believe in the laws of prosperity! It seemed to me that anybody could be prosperous charging such amounts. It wasn't even very difficult for them to hold up $50 notes and burn them, as some of them did, seeing that they had maybe $20,000 coming in for the workshop. I began to wonder to what extent these people were just talking about prosperity and how much they actually believed in it.

It was then, in the mid-70s, that I decided to work for the rest of my life—as I then assumed—on a donation basis. And as I began to work with the 'rules' of echo-nomics—'as you give out, so it comes back'—I realised this involved facing my fears. As an accountant I had charged a phenomenal amount for my time because I was 'professional'. Now, instead, I was sitting in front of audiences talking about prosperity for whole weekends for no set fee at all. People would come up to me afterwards, hug me and tell me I was fantastic—and I would have to pay the rent of the hall myself. It really faced me with the question of whether I was the victim or the master of the situation. Was I willing to keep on giving out? And would it come back?

As I wound up my business and moved into doing prosperity workshops full-time, I began to realise just how it works: providing I keep giving out, somehow the money comes. I don't have to expect it back from any specific person or organisation. I don't have to go to someone and say, "By the way, do you know what I've just given you? Do you know I have a bill to pay tomorrow?" No, it comes in extraordinary ways, such as from somebody I haven't seen for five years who writes: "I realised my life changed when you said who I was and what I could become, when you reminded me of my own beauty. Suddenly I had the overwhelming feeling to send you this amount of money."

Of course, for anything to be able to 'come back' to you, you have to be able to receive—and another thing I had to face was my unwillingness to do this. One day a woman came into my office and put $30 on my desk. "What's that for?" I asked.

"It's for you."

"Oh," I said, "we're just about to publish a little book. We can put it towards that."

"It's for you," she said.

"We've started a donation box for the centre. We can stick it in there."

"It's for *you*."

"I tell you what. We're going to invite a visiting speaker over next year. We'll put it towards his fare."

"It's for *you*."

Then she left. My shirt was soaking, I was bright as a beetroot and my fingers were dripping wet. This was from a female woman and I was brought up in England where you didn't get gifts like that from women. But she played her part beautifully. She gave me the opportunity to face my fear and then to begin to relax and open up, to allow something to happen. We hear about these rules such as 'as you give out, so it comes back', but are we prepared to face the fears involved? This gets us back to the relationships between employers and employees and the unemployed, between the north and south of the planet, and to all those other problems facing us in our society. Behind them all is a massive fear. We play our part when we face our fear and start doing something. It can be very difficult but always, I believe, people come along to give us the opportunities and the support.

There is also a kind of 'plastic echo-nomics' where people make *sure* things come back to them. It's the manipulative part of our society— constant unnecessary extended credit or undue charging of fees or powerful organisations taking more and more from each other. Even people who consider themselves part of the new age fool themselves in this respect. "Of course I'm part of the new," they say, while polishing their haloes. But there are some wonderful examples of plastic echo- nomics among new age people—the development of chain letters, for example, where the people who take part convince themselves that this is some sort of spiritual speciality that will bring prosperity to people who are in need. And then there is networking. In essence it is a magnificent concept, but I have so often seen it distorted by people tak- ing advantage of others: someone knocks at a stranger's door, for instance, on the strength of a distant link with some group or mutual acquaintance and expects to be fed and entertained for several weeks.

The essence of plastic echo-nomics, whether in business or other situations, is one of taking.

Business itself can actually be a beautiful process of expansion, of people interacting and enjoying being together, watching a dream come into being and seeing a service that can be provided. There are some magnificent, beautiful, caring people in business and government doing fantastic jobs. The qualities of the next economy, in my opinion, are information, communication, cooperation and living together. There's nothing wrong with business itself; it's just that we don't always bring these qualities into it.

For instance, people are constantly trying to overcome the need to pay other people, entering into legal processes where they can't be got at. But when they stop paying, they also stop communicating. Credit managers are constantly trying to get people on the phone and instead drawing a blank which finally ends in a huge legal process. I so often tell groups who have gone through financial difficulties that the most important thing is to make a commitment to begin to pay off their debts. Once they do that and start with even a small amount of repayment, they are astounded at how things begin to work out for them. They have broken the cycle of running out on each other.

Another example is tax evasion, which many people get caught up in. Sometimes in seminars I suggest that people start to love paying taxes, and usually a sick laugh goes round the audience. We have reached a point of believing that taxes are our enemy. But not paying taxes can cause tremendous stress because we cut ourselves off from working with the whole. We separate ourselves from the nation and the world to which we belong.

When I was in America a few months ago people kept coming up to me and talking about mega-this and mega-that. Some of them seemed to use it every second word. I found myself thinking that we have to be very careful of getting caught up in always looking for something big. After these people told me all their megas, they would ask what I did. I would say, "I'm a very simple person"—and that normally ended the conversation! We don't have enough simple conversations. We so often believe we have to get involved in big-people stuff that we've lost the ability to just be simple and enjoy where we are. When we look at some of the most magnificent and humane projects and businesses of service that exist, we realise how many of them were started in a simple way, by people who weren't going for big but who were successful because they just lived in the moment. We so often try to forecast what it's going to be like in ten or twenty years time, whereas the only thing we can be certain of is that if we really knew what was going to happen in the next ten years, most of us would shoot ourselves. With the world changing so rapidly, we are not at this moment aware of how we will be equipped to handle what is coming up.

Yet when we look back over the last ten years and think of the devastation some of us have worked through—the broken relationships, companies collapsing, times when we lost all we owned and loved and thought would bring us happiness—nonetheless here we are now, happy, laughing people with an excitement in our hearts, who have something often so much more valuable than we had ten years ago. So I feel it's important not to do too much forecasting, because it is in today that the opportunities lie; it is in this moment that we can discover how to handle the coming decade and build the new economy. Each individual holds part of that plan. Often when we get an idea we feel we have to rush around and tell everybody about it. But nobody can hear until they are ready to hear, and when they are ready to hear, they've already got it. When we feel we have to go on a mission around the world we are missing so much of the point, because it is now, where we are, that we need to be, acting and demonstrating—doing an Albert Schweitzer in other words.

I do a lot of work with people with degenerative illnesses. Recently I held a seminar for diabetics and invited a friend who is a brilliant dietician to speak. That day, instead of talking about various foods and what they contain, she talked about obesity and all the funny habits diabetics in the the audience might have—how they might pretend they are eating only a little but at the same time go to great lengths to get a lot of food inside them. Eventually she invited questions, but not a hand went up. She had done the unforgivable: she had talked about people, about us. But that is what we have to do now. It is so easy to talk about the rest of the world, about all the strange things other people are doing and why they aren't working. We are always saying: "If only employees would work harder, if only employers would pay more, if only those people in Third World countries would stop breeding ... everything would be great; my future would be assured." But it doesn't work that way. It comes back to looking at ourselves constantly and realising that every time we break through a limitation, we move closer to the vision we could have for everybody—and above all we come closer to the security we so deeply desire.

When I give seminars on prosperity I mention the power of affirmations and how people who are caught up with all the bad things that are happening can move their thinking to the positive. When I ask people to repeat the affirmation, "My financial affairs are in perfect order now," they roar with laughter. They seem to believe that their financial affairs are not in perfect order. This highlights the strange relationship we have with money. Recently I got a call from an acquaintance who told me that he was now president of an organisation that sounded like an extraordinarily big and powerful group consisting of top people from universities, hospitals, colleges and businesses. Then he said, "We're putting out a newsletter and, knowing the work the Relaxation Centre does in the community, we wondered if you'd like to pay for it." I was astounded. I experienced, as I often do, almost a cry inside me: "Where is humanity at? How can all these people on very large salaries possibly see themselves as so lacking that they have to call somebody like me to subsidise them?"

Affirming abundance is such an important aspect of the new economy. 'Lack' thinking isn't just in the Third World; it's in us too, right here in the society of abundance and enormous wealth. We're locked in feelings and thoughts of lack—and this contributes greatly to the lack manifesting in Third World countries. Most people think the word abundance means total overflowing, whereas it is a magnificent word that says everything is there in perfect timing and proportion to what one needs. It's very exciting to realise that we are part of a universe that can supply us perfectly.

Sometimes people tell me that I can't expect poor people to believe this. But I'm not so worried about poor people in this regard; I'm interested in all the people who have got so much yet who are thinking lack, because many of them are the effective leaders of our society and the ones who are setting the scene. It has been estimated that the direction the world goes in is set by about only 5% of its total population and the other 95% basically follow suit. If that 5% begin a shift, the dynamic effect on the rest of the world can be enormous. It has also been said that when one man or woman changes, the whole world changes. We tend to come up with excuses for not changing, but we have to decide whether we are masters of ourselves and want to begin to explore the potential for a new economy or whether we're just going to sit back and wait for the rest of the world to change first.

I feel passionately that we are moving towards an age both of oneness and of personal responsibility. When we look into the world we see that there are more people drawing social security and pensions than ever before—and let's remember that there is nothing wrong with those payments; it's for each individual to decide whether they need them or whether they can move beyond them and not get stuck with them. But all the major governments have estimated that by the year 2000 they will not be able to maintain social security payments. That's going to involve a big shift in our thinking.   *U.S. house matters—pay*

who has the It is time to take full responsibility for unemployment. Many of the unemployed are people who have entered a cycle they don't understand and have tried in vain to break out of it. All of us need compassion, not blame, from time to time, to hear people say, "I'm with you. I can hear you." There are ways to move beyond these problems; there *must* be ways, because while there is a single human being on this planet there is a new way to be discovered. I think we are moving towards finding those new ways and towards working *together* rather than having some people consider themselves bosses and others employees. Working together can break down those barriers; allow us to sit with those we work with and share how we feel. It's how families should be. Sometimes people comment how wonderful it would be to live in a community. I often reply that it would be wonderful to live happily in a family, because the family is a community and so many people find it challenging, especially as things are changing so rapidly—as teenagers do different things from what they used to, as women alter their roles and so on. One of the most important things we have to do is to develop quality time between us. The average father in the United States spends only 43 seconds per day quality time with his child—that's when they are really together with the TV off. The need for quality time applies to our work life too. How much quality time do we spend with the people we work with, especially those who seem to belong to a different part of the work force? How often are we prepared to sit listening to them and really hearing what they are trying to say? Or do we wait until people reach the point where they go on strike and try to destroy the organisation?

Sometimes in my talks with business groups I mention what I call the Three 'Rs'. These have been the basis of many of the great strikes that have happened. First of all, somebody resents something and then they resist it. The response from 'the other side' is, "Oh, they're not getting away with that," and they take revenge of some kind, even if it is just a nasty word or facial expression. The person who started the cycle now resents *this*, resists it, thinks, "They're not getting away with that one," and takes revenge. Gradually it works up the scale to the point where you can have the whole country on strike because of something as trivial as a dirty towel in a washroom. All this could be avoided if only we spent more quality time with one another and made sure we listened to each other.

Paul Hawken, the author of *The Next Economy*, talks about moving from the mass economy into the informative economy, in which quality is a keynote. When we have quality with one another, we can also have quality with ourselves, and that results in quality products. As we begin to move away from seeing things only as they relate to size, power and quantity, we will come into an understanding of the extraordinary power that derives from quality; and when we touch into quality, then we begin to understand our own strength and that of our community and our planet. At that moment we discover love; not a gushy emotional process but the love of people who care—and our world screams out for people who care.

Altogether I am full of positive anticipation for the world we're going into. I believe we're right on target. And we must remember that it is very important not to condemn anything that has happened in the past, either in our own lives or in the world we have come through. Our parents, the schools we went to, the things we learnt—everything has been perfect for bringing us to this particular point. It is vital that we don't get caught up in the feeling that some things should never have happened or that we were being 'bad' when we did certain things. But we don't need to take the past into the future. We must start living now, discover what is appropriate for the present and be excited about each day as it comes along.

When I look at all the 'dreadful' things needing to be put right in our society, I see a magnificent lot of God-given opportunities. I even wonder if God gave them to us, or if we gave them to ourselves, because everybody loves a challenge—that's what life is about. The greatest enjoyment comes when we've broken through a challenge. Without these challenges, what would we be doing? They are the doorways for every one of us to go through and find meaning for ourselves. Every individual can do this and that is the important thing: feeling the power to do. For me that is life and it's very exciting.

Politics and the New Economics

Jonathon Porritt

Jonathon Porritt, Director of Friends of the Earth in Britain, is an articulate and inspiring representative of the whole Green movement. He is a leading member of the British Ecology Party and author of **Seeing Green: The Politics of Ecology Explained**.

What I would like to do here is to look at the relationship between the new economics and conventional politics, and at what it is about conventional politics that has such a problem with the new economics. To do this I will need to suggest something of what the new economics might be, so I am going to attempt to summarise it in ten simple points. I acknowledge that this is an almost impossible task. Whole conferences have deliberated on the question, countless people are worried about it, and more books than you can imagine have been written about it. Nevertheless, I am going to try to determine some of the principles that go with the new economics. The list I will draw up is in order of controversy, so the first bits will, I hope, be acceptable to everybody. The bits at the bottom are where you can start walking out.

The first principle of the new economics is that of small scale. This notion has become part of the mythology of the new economics and of the whole Green movement, partly because of the debt we owe to Fritz Schumacher, and partly because all of us, I suspect, understand that the scale of things is extremely important. Conventional politicians and economists have several problems with this notion, both at the practical and conceptual levels of modern-day politics. As far as the left are concerned, they derive most of their power from their base within organised mass labour, particularly through the unions; while for the Tories, big business and multi-nationalisation of the world economy are practically the *sine qua non* of economic wealth. Both are used to thinking in terms of macro-economics, so the idea that the whole economy might be based on a small scale understanding of economic wealth is very upsetting.

Linked with this is the idea that small scale needs to be decentralised. This is also a considerable threat to conventional politicians and economists, for whatever end of the scale you look at, it seems to take their power away from them. The nicest form of centralised politics that we have in Britain today is the kind of paternalism characterised by the better part of the Labour Party and the Alliance. The worst is the kind of quasi-totalitarian approach towards today's difficulties that we find in certain parts of the Tory Party, as well as in many other countries. Essentially, centralised politics operates from the notion that politicians know best, that they alone are in a position to distribute benefits to the poor, benighted population, and that this population could not possibly get on without them. And whether you go for the paternalist or the quasi-totalitarian approach, nothing could be more threatening than the idea of decentralising the whole current political system and power base.

The third principle is one that I broadly call work, rather than jobs. We are moving away from an economy where we can talk about creating x-hundred thousand or x-million *jobs* to an economy where we talk about the *work* people do, whether it be in the formal economy, the informal economy, the voluntary economy, the black economy or whatever. The most important thing to realise about this is the point that Hazel Henderson first raised, which is as follows: at the moment the wealth of society is distributed through the work that people do in that society. By and large that is how the cake of our wealth, of our GNP, is divided up. People who don't have jobs are given the crumbs, something to tide them over until such time as they do have a job. But once we separate out the distribution of wealth from the work that people do, we move into an entirely different economy. And it is an economy that is desperately upsetting to conventional politicians, because one of the means by which they retain power over the electorate is their ability—or inability, depending on the way you look at it—to provide jobs for them. So this shift is not just a cosmetic one at all, even though in many respects it will not actually involve any great revolutionary implications for the economy.

I haven't got time here to talk about the quality of work, but as you know conventional politics doesn't acknowledge the question of quality of work, so I'll pass over that quite quickly.

The fourth point is the shift from surfeit to sufficiency—from the politics of more and more towards the politics of enough. This again strikes absolutely at the heart of conventional politics, which, if you strip it down to its bare essentials, is no more than an assembly of different people standing up on different platforms and offering a different range of goodies to the assorted masses. The idea is that one selection of goodies, one shopping list, is better than the others, and if you vote for me, I will be able to give you this. It has become part and parcel of post-war politics that practically the only way in which a conventional politician dares to offer himself or herself to the electorate is in terms of promising more. The notion of sufficiency rather than surfeit is therefore deeply challenging to conventional politicians because it takes away from them the means by which they summon up the courage to offer themselves for election in the first place.

Moving on from that is the notion of international equity. We need to talk about sufficiency not only for ourselves but also for everybody on the planet. This is a very simple concept for Greens, and I think it has to be stressed time after time that Green politics is not something exclusively relevant to modern, industrialised Western countries but is something that applies equally to all countries across the globe. It *has* to apply equally because there is no way that Green politics can work in one part of the globe without working in the rest. Similarly, the new economics can only be relevant to one part of the planet by being relevant to the rest of it, because it derives its inspiration equally from our knowledge of and sympathy for the Third World as from concern for our own people. By and large, conventional politicians today have, despite a certain twitching of their conscience, dismissed the Third World from their concern. They are in the business of winning power, so they pander to the majority of the electorate, who, to put it bluntly, don't give a stuff for the Third World.

Sixthly, and pushing the boat out even further and more distressingly for contemporary politicians, is the notion of what the Americans so wonderfully call intergenerational equity. This is quite a simple concept—that the redistribution of wealth does not apply exclusively to one generation or one people at one time. It must apply over the course of generations, so that all people to come, as yet unborn, have an equal share of the Earth's wealth. Frankly, this is the point at which contemporary politics completely parts company with what we are saying. It is possible—though difficult—for contemporary politicians to cope with the first five criteria. But this notion is too much for them. The reason is quite simply that the business of staying in power entails exclusive concentration on a short time scale—the next span of parliament, the next length of time they are in office—and the idea of pitching their horizons a bit further than that is very difficult for them.

The seventh point is the idea of a participatory approach to the creation of wealth. This is actually a very challenging concept. It is unfortunately true to say that conventional socialism today has succeeded only by creating a client body 'out there', while contemporary capitalism has succeeded only by creating a passive set of consumers 'out there'. Both major political parties in Britain today depend on that passivity in their audience, in the people they claim to serve. So the notion of participatory economics in which all people equally share the responsibility of wealth creation is a very significant political challenge.

The eighth point is that of the feminine principle. In a world organised entirely according to masculine principles, the idea of our economics responding first and foremost to the feminine principle is more than challenging to contemporary politicians, it is something they literally have to close down on entirely. The point where you can most easily spot a contemporary politician is when you talk about the feminine principle—their eyes glaze over, be they man or woman, and they begin to think you have moved into some transcendental scenario that has no relevance whatsoever to the immediate needs of the people they think they represent.

Ninthly, the new economics is not class based. It does not appeal uniquely to one class or sector in society. Now, an interesting question that has come up is whether one of the reasons the new economics has not succeeded is because there is no class backing for it. Is the slow growth of the new politics or the new economics a consequence of not having a class interest built into it? I'm not sure. I suspect that in the long run this will actually become a tremendous liberation as regards winning support rather than a block or constraint.

Lastly is the notion that the new economics is biocentric. What this means is that over and above the human component we need to stress the planetary component or the notion of life on Earth. This has a huge philosophical consequence. Most of us live in societies and according to rules that are anthropocentric. They are determined and regulated by those who see the human species as being not only dominant but so dominant that they have the right to control all the rest of life on Earth. The new economics, I suggest, involves shifting our philosophical base away from an anthropocentric notion towards a biocentric or life-centred appreciation of wealth.

Now, if these ten principles do indeed approximate to a description of the new economics, the challenge they entail in hard, pragmatic, political terms is enormous. To expect conventional political parties to accommodate themselves to this set of principles is really asking for a great deal. These principles have profound political implications and if we remain unaware of them we condemn ourselves to impotence.

So where do we go from here? Conventional politicians and economists—I throw this out as a thesis—are incapable of accommodating themselves to these principles fast enough to make enough of a difference. Some of you might say, "Ditch politics entirely. It is not the political parties in particular that are at fault, be they left or right or centre, but the very business of politics itself. Let us revert to an anarchist model, a breakdown of community into more or less autonomous groups, and move away from the notion of party politics as being the base of society to rely more on decentralist principles." However, I have little sympathy with this view. I have waged a long campaign against what I call manic minisculism within the Green movement. People who seriously believe that a combination of sporadic and arbitrary decentralised initiatives can actually provide answers for all people on this planet are severely fooling themselves. There is a romantic—almost illusory—attachment to the notion of complete decentralisation that lurks at the back of a lot of Green and alternative thinking, and I believe it renders them incapable of serious political or social analysis. We are looking for something else.

No doubt you are expecting me to say, "Aha! That only leaves Green politics as the answer." Well, possibly. I could have said definitely, but I recently ceased to be co-chair of the Ecology Party, so now I can say possibly. I say possibly, actually, for genuine reasons, because I do not at the moment think that, as it is presently constituted, Green politics provides the answer either.

Incidentally, I am a bit concerned about the way in which politicians today are attempting to use the word Green. You might think that we in the Ecology Party would be thrilled to hear Tories, Socialists, Liberals and SDP-ites all leaping to their feet and saying, "We represent Green concerns. Come and vote for us." Well, we're not, and the reason is because they are using the word Green in the old-fashioned sense to refer to reformist environmentalism. Now that is not what Green politics is about. It does not deal with only academic ecological issues and conservation. It deals with a whole gamut of social and economic issues.

24

The reason I say Green politics doesn't provide the whole answer yet is that up until now we have unfortunately failed to articulate our politics in such a way that reaches a broad enough range of people. We have talked eloquently and passionately about how we believe it necessary to respond to the problems on the planet, to respond to the needs of other species, the needs of the Third World and the needs of generations as yet unborn. And credit is due to those who deliberately take those interests on board and attempt to represent them in the political forum. Yet we have also neglected one of the major aspects of politics, which is to represent the interests of ordinary people alive today. There has been a very definite elitist tendency in Green politics which has pretended that we can put the more immediate, material concerns of people to one side in the interests of serving the planet better.

Every time we would come up with our ecotopian vision of the future, people would say, "It sounds wonderful. But to do it you're going to have to change human nature." This was considered the ultimate rebuttal of the Green alternative—it was a great set of ideas, but it failed to take into account one fundamental aspect, namely human nature. The unwritten assumption behind this argument is that human nature is fixed, that it is inherently destructive and basically tends towards evil rather than good. I myself tend towards the view that sees human nature as being free and unfixed by any predetermined set of values.

However, even if you believe that human nature has a potential for change, you still have to face the incontrovertible and extremely ugly fact that most people in our society today do not care about the interests of the planet, of the Third World or often even of their children and grandchildren. That brings us front up against the element of self-interest in people, and the extent to which it thwarts all our ideals and goals. Those who choose to disregard the element of self-interest in politics—be it conventional politics or Green politics—are seriously deluding themselves. There is no magic carpet to some new ecotopian world. If we are to move down the road we all need to—and I believe we shall indeed do this—we have to confront the grittiest parts of human nature.

That is a ruthlessly pragmatic analysis of society today, and after eight years in the Ecology Party I can tell you that you have no option *but* to be ruthlessly pragmatic. It has taken me a long time to get my mind and tongue and my whole way of looking at life around the concept of self-interest. I tend to float at a somewhat generalised, abstract level, and it was an enormous problem to realise that the thing I was completely failing to deal with was the element of self-interest.

Now, one of the things the new economics is beginning to teach the Green movement is a way in which we might reach out to a broader audience. It involves the honest acceptance of self-interest as an aspect of economics. We are realising that we can actually demonstrate in *our* economic terms (which rely partly on conventional economics and partly on the economics *we* find to be important) that the costs of doing things in the industrial way are greater than the benefits which we are meant to enjoy as a result. It's conventional cost/benefit analysis; weighing up the costs and weighing up the benefits. We can also demonstrate that the implications of *not* realising that we live on a finite planet are so devastating that any politician or economist who fails to take them into account is in the business of fooling the electorate or fooling themselves.

What we need to do is to look at the principles of the new economics and see how we can articulate them in such a way as to meet people's immediate self-interest, rather than to meet a set of somewhat transcendental goals or ideals. Is there more in our shopping list—conventionally measured for ordinary people—than there is in the shopping list of ordinary politicians? Now, that may sound to you so appalling a betrayal of the idealism of Green politics that you may wish to have no part in such a process. "Who is he," you may say, "to criticise conventional politicians for putting forward shopping lists which offer people more, and then to go ahead and do exactly the same?" You have a point. Politics is by definition, in my opinion, a very unpleasant business. But it seems to me that we have to acknowledge some of the inherent problems of politics in our attempt to articulate the new economics. In putting this position to you so bluntly, I am hoping to bring you up against the reality of what is involved in changing political beliefs in a society such as ours. However, the notion of the synthesis between idealism and self-interest may not in fact be totally appalling. Let me attempt to demonstrate this by reading one paragraph from my book, *Seeing Green* (it took me hours to write this paragraph and I can't honestly pretend to say it all over again).

"At the individual level today, wealth means the visible symbols of affluence. It means consumer durables and credit cards and being rich enough to have a huge overdraft. How oh how is this going to change in the new order? In a sustainable, ecological future, the wealthy will be those who have the independence and the education to enhance the real quality of their lives. The poor will be those who look back to an age where money might—but never quite did—buy happiness. The wealthy will be those who live and work in friendly, mutually supportive communities. The poor will be those still trucking off to cities in crowded commuter trains to do jobs they can't stand anyway. The wealthy will be those who make more of their own entertainment in a more convivial society. The poor will be twiddling the buttons on their cable-TV videos, trying to find the right brand of oblivion. The wealthy will be growing as much of their own food as they can, and growing it organically. The poor will be paying through the nose for an adulterated mess of pottage. The wealthy will be re-using and recycling and taking pride in how long things last and how easy they are to repair. The poor will be wondering when the novelty went out of novelty. The wealthy will be fully involved in their parish or neighbourhood council, getting things done for themselves and for their community. The poor will still be blaming the government. Wealth in both its physical and its spiritual dimension will have regained its true meaning."

I came to think about wealth in these terms largely through reading the works of R.H. Tawney, one of the greatest of all socialist thinkers and a model and inspiration to us today. The quote that triggered my thinking was this: "The most obvious facts are the most easily forgotten. Both the existing economic order and too many of the projects advanced for reconstructing it break down through their neglect of the simple truth that since even quite common people have souls, no increase in material wealth will compensate them for arrangements which insult their self-respect and impair their freedom." This is an astonishingly important statement. However much we look to the advantages of our materialist age, if we ride roughshod over the spiritual element of human nature we actually create the situation in which poverty flourishes rather than the kind of wealth on which we depend.

While I was sitting in the auditorium this morning somebody got up and said that the symbols of the Aquarian Age are water and air. That got me thinking, and I would like to give you an Aquarian analogy or approach to the new economics. I'm not sure that air would be my second symbol—I like to keep my feet on mother Earth—but there we are.

When I was about eight, my parents took me out on holiday to Jamaica, where we stayed in an extremely luxurious tourist resort called

Ocho Rios, which means eight rivers. I had seen rivers converging and had been enormously impressed, so I was fascinated by the notion of eight rivers coming together. I kept pestering my father to take me to see them. Eventually he fobbed me off with some tourist guide, who in fact was extremely reluctant to go, and we duly trucked off about 15 miles to the *real* village of Ocho Rios. As we got closer to the place where these eight rivers were supposed to converge, the guide got more and more apologetic. "It's the summer," he said. "All the rivers have dried up. They don't really exist any more; some have gone underground."

When we arrived, there was one of the most tawdry and disgusting sights I have ever seen. A fairly large Jamaican woman was defecating copiously on the site where these eight rivers were said to converge, and all around her was the debris of the Coca-colonisation of Jamaican life. There was hardly any water to be seen anywhere. I must admit it was quite a difficult experience. "Is that it?" I asked the guide. "Yes," he said. "That's where the rivers *used* to flow together."

In the Ecology Party we talk a lot about the wasteland of contemporary economics. Now, it occurs to me that this model of eight rivers could be used to describe the various streams which could in fact be nourishing our society. Some of them are spiritual, others are pragmatic or political. But all of them have dried up or have become dammed, so that the potential sources of nourishment for our society are not contributing the wealth that they could, and this is why we have a wasteland today.

The first of these rivers is what I would call the deist religions—those faiths which believe in a godhead of some kind. But people have for so long worried about which words to say over which stream according to which dogma, that the river has actually dried up and disappeared while they have been talking, and they haven't even noticed it. The second river is that of the animist or pagan religions, those which believe that we are in some way spiritually involved in the Earth and dependent on our relationship with her. To some extent, these have always been represented by fairly small streams running through the mainland of contemporary society, but they have not always been pure—indeed, some of them have been very corrupt, and many people have been put off by the nude bodies of those cavorting around on their banks.

The third main river is that of the secular humanist tradition. I would also classify this as spiritual, in the sense that there are non-religious understandings of the spirit that are very important for the maintenance of humankind.

In terms of pragmatic politics we have what I loosely refer to as conventional politics. Here we have the two rivers of left and right. The river of the left is basically drawing its water from an aquifer which has long since been exhausted. Personally, I think that aquifer was once the sweetest and purest source of wealth and inspiration to society, but it has undoubtedly run dry and has ceased to serve the people in the way it used to. The river of the right has been privatised: you can only get to it now if you can pay to find your way to it—and then you have to pay for the water you take from it. The river of the right has ceased to serve the interests of all people living in society.

The sixth river is the apolitical one, consisting of a score of different movements such as the feminist, environmentalist and peace movements, which don't operate in the conventional political world but which nonetheless have fed the mainstream of society in many different ways. Unfortunately, they have increasingly developed such vociferous tendencies to serve only their own interests that they have ceased to understand the need to irrigate the common ground of the whole of society.

The seventh river is that of business. Now, business has undoubtedly brought great wealth to society at different times, and has enormously benefited people's lifestyles and material living standards, and I do not think it worthwhile to criticise business as the means by which all things have been corrupted. Unfortunately, however, it has become obsessed with itself rather than with serving the needs of people, and to that extent the water flowing into society from the world of business has been severely polluted, often with our own waste products. It is now harder and harder for business to bring the source of wealth to our society.

The eighth river is that of technology, and this has been dammed off for years—dammed literally by its obsession with large-scale technology and damned metaphorically by its obsession with nuclear technology.

The challenge facing the new economics, as I see it, is to free up these various rivers so that they can once again flow to serve humankind. And things are, in fact, beginning to move. The deist tradition is now having to acknowledge, as in the liberation theology argued in South America, that the words of Christ are real political directives that those who claim to be Christians must follow through in their own lives. There is a greater awareness of the value of what the animist and pagan traditions have to offer, and the sensationalism has become less. Conventional politics is shifting—even if only at the cosmetic level at present—as people begin to acknowledge the imperatives of a finite planet; while those people who operate apolitically are increasingly sharing a sense of their common ground. There are trends in business which indicate it is starting again to serve the needs of people rather than the needs of abstract imperatives such as profitability or productivity, while technology now has the potential to serve all these different streams and to make them possible by emphasising the small scale, the decentralised and the energy-efficient.

Everybody involved in the new economics is, I believe, in some way a prophet. We are putting forward a revolutionary set of ideas to a people who have become unaccustomed to the notion of a different way of doing things. What this requires from us is the willingness to get our hands dirty doing the things we claim to believe in, not standing apart telling other people what to do. It requires us first and foremost to recognise that each of the rivers feeding our society is as valuable as the others, and that it is only by working together that we can make our Earth flourish again for the benefit of all people.

Part II

The Next Economy:
Work, Industry and Business

The Changing Shape of Work

Charles Handy

*Economist, writer, former oil executive and visiting professor at the
London Business School, Charles Handy offers some positive
possibilities for the future of work in our society as well as redefining
many aspects of the current economic system. He is author of several
books, including* **The Future of Work**.

Not long ago I asked an Irishman how to get somewhere and he didn't
say, as all Irishmen are supposed to, "I wouldn't start from here."
What he said was, "Go down the road there, and after a mile or so
you'll come to an old ruined church on the right-hand side of the road
opposite a dark wood. Half a mile before you get there, turn left up the
hill." That may sound like a typical Irish road direction, but actually
it's the story of the talk I want to give you. I want to describe the road
along which the work and money patterns in our society are going. My
worry is that if we don't go left up the hill before we get to the end of
that road, we will find ourselves at a very ruined church and a very
dark wood. To put it another way, I think I bring you news of some
exciting possibilities in today's economy, some hopeful signs and glimmers for the next economy. But they are like little lamps flickering in
the darkness: they could easily go out with a puff of the wrong kind of
wind.

As an Irishman, I can be totally dispassionate about the English, and
it seems to me that in this matter as in so many others, the English are
stumbling backwards into the future. It's a posture which the English
like because it allows them to look longingly at the past while they
gradually retreat from it. The only trouble is that they may end up on
their backs in a pothole if they're not careful.

Let me start by giving you four statistics. The first is that the work
force in Britain—or at least the population of working age—is going to
grow by one million people over the next 15 years, despite the falling

birthrate and the fact that schools are closing because we don't have enough 16-year-olds to fill them. The reason for this is that although we are producing fewer people from our schools and colleges, they still total more than the number of people in their 60s who are leaving, dying or retiring (because we killed a lot of that older generation in the last war). Most industrial countries are in a similar position. OECD reckons that we are going to have to create 20,000 new jobs every day just to keep pace with the new workers joining the work force. Unemployment isn't going to go away.

Secondly, in the 20 years between 1961 and 1981, unemployment in this country rose dramatically by 2.2 million, while the number of working wives increased by 2.7 million. I am not suggesting that women caused unemployment: in fact, many of them went into totally different jobs than those that men came out of. However, it is clear that the work force has quite dramatically become more feminine in the last 20 years, even though most of those women have gone into part-time jobs.

Thirdly, in this country today—and I suspect in most European countries—one out of every two people of working age and available for work (ie, between the ages of 16 and 65, and not in school, university, hospital or prison) is not now in a full-time conventional job. They are not all unemployed, of course, though regrettably three million odd are. Many more are employed part-time—nearly five million at present, with their numbers growing rapidly. Many are self-employed; 2.5 million officially, more unofficially, and their numbers are also growing rapidly. Then there is another group of 3.5 million people who the OECD nicely and I think accurately call 'unpaid domestic workers'. We know what sex most of them are—people who have not registered for work but who are in a real sense 'working'. All these categories add up to just over 14 million, which is 46% of the 31 million people currently available for work. The point is that the idea that our society can still look to providing jobs for everybody has long ago become a mistaken one. For some time now it has not been true to say to children in our schools, "Each of you is going to have a job in a good society." Only one out of two is going to be in what we normally call a conventional full-time job. The world has changed quite fast.

The last of the four statistics is that in the past 20 years we have halved the length of the life-time job expectancy almost without noticing it. When I left university I expected to go to work for roughly 47 hours a week for 47 weeks a year for 47 years, which multiplies out to around 100,000 hours (102,000 actually). We have now split that to 50,000 hours for somebody leaving school or college today. You will say don't be ridiculous—even in lazy old Britain we work more than 23½ hours a week and 23½ weeks a year. But mathematics is a baffling science, and according to cube law 37 × 37 × 37 equals 50,000. Or, to put it another way, 35 hours a week for 45 weeks a year for 32 years equals 50,000. In fact, we are almost there already. These days it is very difficult to get into the full-time work force before you are 20. If you are middle-class and successful you go to university and you have your year in India with a guitar, or you go to some place like the Findhorn Foundation for three years and then join the work force. If you are not middle-class and successful you join the Youth Training Scheme for one year and then have three years with a bad guitar in the back streets of Brixton or Liverpool. Most people can't get into the work force before they are in their early 20s. In addition, more and more people are now leaving the work force in their 50s. If you ask someone of 30 today how he or she looks forward to working in a particular organisation in 30 years' time, they look at you with horror and say, "What? Still in this organisation when I'm 60? No way." Nor will organisations be able to afford it. Already people are in the work force from roughly 20 to 52, 53 years of age—a total of 32 years. We have halved the job.

The questions of what we are going to do with the extra 50,000 hours and what we are going to live on are extraordinarily interesting and have some exciting possible answers, which I will come back to later. But first I want to tell you what many organisations are doing under the current pressures. First of all, they are substituting capital for labour. The basic reason for the contraction of the job and the working life is that labour has been priced pretty high. The way to reduce costs in an organisation if you can't get the wage rate down is to reduce the number of people employed and to substitute capital instead. So today we have what I call the combine harvester phenomenon. In my youth in Ireland, there would be lots and lots of people harvesting the wheat or oats in the fields, with a threshing machine in the corner, and harvest suppers to follow the work. Now one man in a great big machine will come along and do the whole lot in one afternoon in August. The combine harvester effect is happening all over in industry today.

Secondly, organisations now have three categories of people working with them. First there is the professional core—people who have the particular skills, knowledge and managerial energy which makes that organisation what it is. They are, as it were, the owners of the organisation's identity. These managers, craftspeople or technical staff are people the organisation cannot do without. It wants them committed, so it binds them to itself with heaps of money, with pension schemes, long-term contracts, fringe benefits, housing help, school fees, career development and long-term security. In return it asks for flexibility and loyalty: "Yes, I will go to such-and-such a place; I will work Sunday afternoons; I won't go home till the office has closed; I'll see it through the night." However, these people are very expensive—increasingly so these days when they want to go round in BMWs instead of Ford Escorts—so the organisation wants to keep them as few as possible.

Increasingly, therefore, organisations are looking to a contractual fringe to do things for them. They start with the cleaning, catering, gardening and chauffeuring, but then go on to include the architects and some of the professional services which could be done as well for them by others as by themselves. They might even look at all the staff services they have in their organisation and ask not only which could be done by other people, but also which could be done by their own people if they pushed them out and turned them into little businesses on their own. In central London today it coste £25,000 to house, feed, water and service a senior executive before you start paying him or her a salary. Therefore it makes sense to call in that executive and say, "We love you dearly. We like your skill and wisdom, but we don't actually need it five days a week every day of the year. We could do with about half of it. So we'll actually pay you your full salary as a *fee* to buy back half of your wisdom and talent if you go out and be an independent business, provided you get out of this building and off our pension fund. Because we'll save £25,000 a year." Organisations are increasingly doing this—and whether it's liberating people or casting them adrift depends on your attitude.

Another thing that organisations need is part-time workers who will work odd hours in small chunks on jobs that have not been automated yet. Many organisations have so much capital tied up in their businesses that they actually want the places to work seven days a week. Hotels already do it; so do airlines, radio stations and television networks, so why shouldn't all organisations? It only makes sense. But the only way it can be done is to have a very flexible labour force that is prepared to work all hours of the day and night in smaller chunks. This flexible labour force is basically part-time, working odd hours on short-term contracts. In many instances in this country, 11 weeks keeps you under the labour legislation: while on less than 16 hours a week you don't have to pay national insurance contributions. Organisations like to keep their costs down. So that's where the growth in the part-time workers is coming in. The interesting thing is that people seem to like it. The General Household Survey, in its analysis of job satisfaction, discovered that the most satisfied workers in our society are part-time women workers. They were so horrified by this finding that they spent three pages trying to explain why the statistics they collected might actually be wrong. It is conceivable, however, that they might be right, and I'll explain why in a moment.

All this adds up to what I think of as the 'Japanese drift'. You may have read marvellous things about Japanese organisations and how they guarantee life-time employment. But I have to tell you that this is guaranteed to only 20% of the work force, the professional core of the large organisations. Only 20% of the Japanese work force is under conditions of life-time employment, and in Japan 'life-time' ends at 55. They have a 32 year working life, just as we are coming to have in this country. After that you're out, and the state pension scheme doesn't start until you are 60. So where do you go? You land up in a very large contractual fringe. All the big Japanese corporations rest on an infrastructure of small sub-contractors. Toyota has 37,500 sub-contractors, and 34,000 of them have less than 100 people working in them. They are tiny family businesses. Japan has 19% of the work force registered as self-employed; in this country we have less than half of that, as do most European countries. Now if you think about it, if you are self-employed you can be poor, broke or out of work, but you can't by logic or by law be *un*employed. Japan has a very large concealed *un*employment in its large *self*-employment, and that's the way we are going now too. There are both good and bad things about that sort of scene.

It is, however, the way you keep yourself flexible. Organisations are exporting their uncertainty into the contractual fringe and the flexible labour force. Marks and Spencers, a marvellous organisation in this country, has no unemployment and no redundancies. But it has a six-week break-clause in all its sweater contracts. Responsibly, it seeks never to operate this, but it could: rather than cut back its work force, it will cut back its orders. So who cuts back the work force? The contractual fringe.

Now what is the result of all this? When you take into consideration the fact that less than half of the population is now in a conventional full-time job, and that the life-time job expectancy is now 50,000 hours, what we are beginning to see, I suggest, is the decline of the *employee society*. There are some exciting possibilities in this. However, for many people, the employee society, for all its faults, has been all that they have known, their only way of getting money and recognition. It is extraordinary that we have people in this country fighting to preserve the right to crawl on their bellies underground hacking coal out of seams, particularly when their fathers were desperate to keep them out of the pits. But the reason they are doing this is because we haven't yet offered any alternative to the employee society: they don't know of any other way in which a decent able-bodied person can earn respectability and contribute to society.

I think there *are* other ways. And here are the glimmers of hope, the exciting possibilities. Let us suppose that 50,000 hours was a norm and not an average. For non-statisticians, the difference is this: an average of 50,000 hours could mean a lot of people having 100,000 hours and a lot of others having none. A norm, on the other hand, means that everybody has 50,000 hours. If everybody had 50,000 hours as a job allowance in life, they could take it in various ways. Some people would work all the hours available from the age of, say, 24 when they were fully educated, becoming part of the professional core until they were around 48; taking their 50,000 hours in one big chunk. Others would choose to spread it more thinly and to work in a job for around 20 hours a week for perhaps 50 or 60 years. Others might sandwich it, taking, say, ten years in the work force and then ten years out of it—to raise a family or have some other experience—and then go back into the work force again. Ironically, this in fact is the way women have always lived. It is also ironic that so many women are now trying to get into the professional core, and that so many men are actually being forced to adopt the way that women have always lived. Our topsy-turvy lives.

A norm of 50,000 hours would mean that everybody had at least another 50,000 hours of normal working life when they would have to do other things than be employed in a conventional job. In my view, the other things would also be work. They would include marginal work, where you do a bit of extra work on the side and charge money for it—turn your hobby into a business, for instance. But because it's marginal, you are therefore able to price it at marginal cost, which allows you to sell your service or product below the market price, and this is good because it increases the economy and brings the price of labour down a little. Then there is 'gift work', where you produce goods and services for other people and don't charge for them. This of course happens all day long in our homes and gardens and communities: we do things we wouldn't dream of charging for.

What I am talking about here is the domestic economy, not the black economy. The black economy is a totally artificial creation, which wouldn't exist if we didn't have tax rates and VAT rates that start so low. There are many people doing perfectly honest marginal businesses on the side who get trapped. If we just raised the tax and VAT rates there wouldn't be a black economy. But the domestic economy is both good and legal. And in labour terms it is half of the economy—the number of hours worked in the domestic economy is estimated to be equal to the number of hours worked in the rest of the economy. It's big business, and it's growing—because if people have more time, then they spend more time doing things for themselves that formerly they paid other people to do.

Now if you have 50,000 hours extra discretionary time, you will spend even more time doing things for yourself and your family and friends that other people would have done—because you will also be a little poorer; you won't have earned so much in life, and the things that people used to do for you are increasingly expensive. And, after all, why shouldn't they be? Recently an American told me about a plumber who presented him with an enormous bill. "Good God, man," he said, "that's as much as I charge as a lawyer." "Sure," said the plumber, "that's what I found out when I was a lawyer."

It is actually cheaper to do things for yourself than pay other people to do them, particularly when you are poorer and have time on your hands. So the domestic economy is likely to grow. I think that's rather good. The Chancellor of the Exchequer thinks it's rather bad, because it doesn't get counted. When you think about it, it is economically disloyal to entertain people at home rather than take them to a restaurant. If you take them to a restaurant, you are creating taxable income and possible employment, so the visible economy grows. And if you entertain them at home with home-grown vegetables, you are even more disloyal, because that again is taking away money from the Chancellor of the Exchequer.

If 50,000 hours was a norm, and we had more of our conventional working lives to spend on our own pursuits, the result is that we would lead what I call 'portfolio lives'. We would have a mix of work at different periods in our lives, a mix of employment or 'job work' with marginal work and gift work. This means that when you ask someone what they do, you may get surprising answers. In the employee society, you get their job title. But in the portfolio society there is no guarantee what they will tell you. The other day I asked a woman what she did. "I write scripts for television," she said. I was greatly impressed because I try to do that, only I never seem to get anywhere. But when she saw me beginning to bow low and bend the knee she said, "Don't worry, they never get accepted." With a sigh of relief I then asked her what she lived on and she said, "I pack eggs on Sunday." Many young people are thinking in a similar way. Recently I met a chap coming down from university. What was he going to do? "Write the great English novel," he said. "Magnificent," I said. "What's it going to be like?" "Henry James," he said. "Oh," I said. "What are you going to live on?" "I'm going to work on a building site," he said, "on Monday and Tuesday afternoons." Flexible labour force. Instrumental relationship with the organisation. Just done for money. But when I asked both these people what they did, they told me not their money work but their gift work—or what they no doubt hoped would become their marginal paid work and maybe eventually their sole income.

People are already living portfolio lives and rejoicing in it when they are young. Will they change when they grow older? I'm not sure. Recently I talked to the deputy headmaster of a comprehensive secondary school, aged 35, who is bothered about education. He and his wife, who also has a job, are resigning and going to live in a small country village where they are going to 'just think and be, play music, read poetry'. "We'll decide in a year or two what we will do," they said. When I was 35 you didn't do that sort of thing. You were hitched into a career and you stayed in it. Today more and more people are moving in and out of jobs because they realise they can count on 50,000 hours of paid employment, but that they will also have 50,000 hours to fill in other ways. The domestic economy is going to flourish and become respectable. It is going to be OK once again to say, "I run the home. I rear children. I look after the old folks. I run the local community hall." Of all the portfolio work I do, the most interesting, exciting and in some ways most status-bearing things are my gift work. If people really press me about what I do, I tell them my voluntary work, because it is the most fun and is what describes me most.

That brings me to what I call 'Micawber lives'. There are two particular aspects about Charles Dickens' Micawber that attract me. The first is his attitude that 'something will turn up, so worry not about the morrow'. Jesus was attributed as saying, "Take no thought for the morrow"; except he was mistranslated. What he actually said was, "Don't get anxious about the morrow." If you are self-employed you can't afford to get anxious about the morrow, because if you do you just go into a flat spin and don't actually do anything. You have to sit loose to the uncertainties of tomorrow. You can't possibly plan your income (as I tell my bank manager) more than three months ahead, so you have to trust in something. It is a very frustrating attitude to live with because there is absolutely no excuse for not doing something you ought to be doing. But it does actually seem to work: something does turn up.

The other thing about Micawber is that he defined happiness as: income 20 shillings and sixpence; expenditure 19 shillings and sixpence: result—happiness. The other way around: result—misery. The point about his philosophy, if you are self-employed, is that happiness is having just a little more money than you need. Now the way to get it is either to make a lot of money or to need less. Paul McCartney apparently used to say, "I think I'll go out and earn a swimming pool today." Well, you don't have to be in the Paul McCartney class to say to yourself, "A holiday in Spain? A thousand pounds? I'll have to go and earn it. But is it worth it? If I don't do the work, I don't have to do the spending." So what you start doing is redefining your needs in a very careful way. This is quite different from the way I thought when I was in employment: *all* I wanted then was more and more money 'just in case'. Then of course when I had that extra money I started spending more of it 'just in case' and also just to keep up with the Joneses and have a video recorder and so on and so forth. If you have to go out and earn a video recorder, you think twice about whether you actually need it or not. And that brings us once again to the domestic economy. If you start to learn to do things yourself, then you don't have to earn the money to pay other people to do them, and then you have a more relaxed life. Micawber comes into his own when portfolio lives and the domestic economy become more dominant.

Another exciting thing about what is happening today is that there is an increased dignity possible in the contractual relationship as opposed to the employee relationship. The contractual fringe is a way of exporting uncertainty, but there is a good side to it as well. People on the contractual fringe, who are not 'employed', are paid not for their time but for their labour; they are paid a fee, not a wage. You pay fees to people who provide services or products, and it doesn't really matter to you whether they provide them by working all night or by working only on Wednesday afternoons or by having their children help them. As long as you get your candle or chair or meal when you want it and of the quality you want it, you pay the fee. It is much more dignified and satisfying, I find, to be paid a fee for something I do or give than having somebody buy my time and then tell me what to do within it. I don't think it is good for anyone to sell their time to other people, and I don't like it. It's a form of economic slavery. Interestingly, the high status occupations in this country—professionals, artists and craftspeople—are all those who charge fees. Fees represent a respect for the individuality and the person behind the work, whereas wages treat you as some kind of human resource.

Organisations today are increasingly dealing in employment *a la carte*. In a sense, they are saying, "Let's find all sorts of ways of relating people to us, but not necessarily by turning them into wage slaves, people whose time we have bought." What happens then is that they end up with organisations of consent, with people there because they want to be there. At the recent Business Network Conference in London, Harvey Jones, chairman of ICI, was describing the way he would like to see his giant commercial organisation in the not-too-far distant future: free persons cooperatively joining together in a variety of different relationships. That is very exciting, because it gets us away from the slavery of the employee society.

It gets more exciting when you think of the new kinds of organisations that this sort of economic order and work relationship could lead to, if we are lucky. It involves what I call the new management. Organisations of the future will be federal, in the sense that they will have small component parts loosely linked together in a large whole to get economies of scale. This is already happening more and more. People in these organisations will talk of tasks, not roles, because the contractual idea of being paid for what you do rather than for your time will work its way through even to the people in the professional core. They will also talk in terms of their particular little group area. People will be working in gangs again, not in lines. This is one of the results of substituting capital for labour, because if capital and the new technology are used effectively, a few people can do what formerly required 100 people to do on a long assembly line—and that liberates them to become autonomous, self-organising groups. It's a much more exciting way of organising.

Organisations are becoming much looser kinds of units in which people see themselves belonging to a family, a gang or a network. Networks and families don't have managers or leaders; they have hubs. They have 'heads' sometimes, but more often they are in some sense self-organising, though I think all networks need a hub. The point is that the management of these families and networks cannot be by autocratic control: it has to be by asking, not telling. You cannot go round telling your colleagues to do this or that. When I moved from business to the university (which is an organisation of consent, full of little families and groups), I started ordering people around, and someone said to me one day, "Charles, you can't tell me to do anything in this place, you know. You can only ask me. The trouble is *I* can tell *you* to go to hell." So the only way of running these organisations with the agreement of the people in them is by asking. It is a very interesting and exciting, though arduous, way of managing because it respects the individuality of all the people in it.

Furthermore, because power is spread around, they have to be run by *empathy*. You have to be able to rely on people to do what you ask them to do, because the controls you are able to exercise over them are limited. If they are in the professional core, they are with you for life. If they are contracting, you don't have any control over what they do outside their own bit of the operation. So you have to trust them to do what you ask them to do. You can only trust people if you understand them, and you can only understand them if you know them. Hence the very great importance that these units are small, and bonded together with some common understanding of what they are all about. If you go around any great organisation and ask people in them what the organisation is about, they will tell you the same thing. They know what they are about because they are bonded together by a common understanding and empathy, and that is the only way of running these sorts of organisations that are growing up. That funny book, *In Search of Excellence*, talks about great businesses in America—they deal with all sorts of extraordinary things like hamburgers and tupperware, but nevertheless they are all well-run organisations. What holds them together is nearly always a common belief in what they are doing. You may think it odd for people to believe in tupperware, but they do: they believe in its quality, and they deeply and sincerely believe that people want excellent tupperware. Now, this is an approach which can be put into the setting of a church, or a voluntary organisation or a school. Recently I have been going round schools and have been dismayed that

42

nobody gives me the same answer when I ask "What does this school stand for?" They haven't actually thought about it; they are just going through their roles.

Management by empathy makes for very exciting organisations, although they are difficult to run. They involve leadership from within, a leadership that finds a common purpose. In addition, in these organisations with small units, development is by growing, not by climbing. They are rather like professional organisations. They don't have many layers—the ladders are very short. If you join an architects' or solicitors' firm—all fee-paid people—you start off as a sort of apprentice, then become an associate and then a partner. If you join a university, you are first a lecturer, then an assistant or associate professor and then a full professor. They are three-layer organisations—and after you get to the third layer you run out of ladders. Like the professional organisations, the new organisations will also need only three layers. It is interesting to discover that there seem to be three layers in the Findhorn Foundation. Now, the point is that once you get to the top layer there is nowhere else to go in terms of climbing ladders, so the hierarchy doesn't mean much. Success then becomes defined as doing the same thing better. It means growing as a person, rather than climbing ladders, and that is very exciting.

Organisations today *have* to get smaller, and yet they also have to be big, to keep the economies of scale. It is interesting to see Findhorn beginning to think, "How can we grow and still stay small?" The answer to this is federalism—but federalism is both difficult and unpredictable. The British have always thought of federalism as a way of keeping their colonies quiet—"If we divide them, things will be all right"—so you find federalism in many of our old colonies and defeated enemies. But it didn't work quite that way, of course. Instead, they got strong, because the parts were strong and interdependent. If the parts are strong and *not* interdependent they go off on their separate ways or fight with each other. We need to structure interdependence into our organisations and communities, so that you can't achieve your common purpose without the help of all the other people. This could make for rather exciting kinds of communities, where people don't just happen to be living in the same place not really needing one another.

In other words, the collapse of the old economic order could lead to the creation of some very exciting organisations as they reform themselves around this new set of possibilities.

However, unless we do something, this is *not* going to happen. I have another scenario, which I have a horrible feeling is a much more realistic one in this country. In this other scenario, we divide the world into primary and secondary labour markets. There are those with nice secure jobs, the professional core, and then there are those who scrub around on the edges, in the black economy, in the contractual fringe with eleven-week contracts, and in the part-time labour force which is exploited by the organisations. Fifty thousand hours then is not the norm; it is not the amount of secure job-employment that everybody is entitled to in their life-time. It is the average. Some people—doctors, professionals and workaholics—have 150,000 hours, while others have none or, if they are lucky, 10,000 hours. Unemployment will grow continuously.

In a rather brilliant science fiction novel called *Gor Saga*, Maureen Duffy sets a story about genetics and its problems in a Britain which I see as becoming totally believable. It is a Britain in which the professionals sit in campus-like surroundings protected by electronic fences, twiddling away with their computers and running an information-controlled world, while outside these campuses live the nons, who are supported by the State and amuse themselves in one way or another on the fringes of society—in shanty towns or in the big cities or in the deserted wildernesses of the country (because we don't need many fields to grow our food). It is a world in which the Churches have to go armed to do good. It is a world, I think, rather like bits of Beirut or, as I thought recently when visiting Northern Ireland, like bits of Belfast. It is a world in which the professionals live in their comfortable suburbs and you need a passport to get into Hampstead.

"Unbelievable," I thought, until two things happened to me recently in the same day. I was talking to a woman who edits books for my publisher and she said, "The future of work is quite plain to me. The world will increasingly be divided into Alphas and Gammas," and she said, flattering me, "You and I will be Alphas and we should be prepared to pay the taxes to keep the Gammas in some comfort, and even to send them to the Costa Brava in Spain twice a year." She thought that was an acceptable and ethical view of the society to come. Then that evening I went out to dinner in Surrey, to one of those private estates that lurk behind the rhododendrums. There was a barrier across the road and I didn't have the plastic card to raise it so I couldn't get in, and I thought, "Aha! Passports for Hampstead!" Maybe it is coming.

This world is one in which there is escalating resentment, in which those who have jobs pay increasingly high taxes to support people who don't do any work at all—and they grudge it. And those who live off the taxes grudge greatly those in jobs driving around in their BMWs and sitting in their campus-like environments. It is a world which could be called a leisured society, but it has the leisure at the bottom of society, not the top. The leisured societies which have worked are those where the leisured classes were at the top, setting values and standards. Societies which have put their leisured classes at the bottom have not lasted long. Bread and circuses, or the modern equivalent of technological equipment, have not pacified people for long. And if you don't have that, in this world of primary and secondary labour forces, you have directed employment. People are sent to put Liverpool to rights, whether they want to go there or not. They are sent to work in the north-east of England, or the north of France, or the wrong part of Belgium, because that is where people and work are needed. A totalitarian existence.

That is the kind of world I see very likely to be coming, rather than the optimistic one—*unless* we do something about it. It is all very well to talk about empowering the individual. It is all right for me to leave the employee society and to go strutting around the stages of the world, hoping that money will come from somewhere. I am privileged, university-educated, with some saleable skills; I can scrape along; life does not have enough hours for me to fill. It is all right for the Cambridge-educated fellow who wants to write the great English novel, or for the woman who writes television scripts. But what about the people leaving the ship-building yards in Sunderland, the people who have been chucked out from the foundries, from the steel mills and the coal mines? Have they got the ability to go round singing for their supper as I do? I doubt it, because they haven't been educated right. I can go on for ages about education. In this country, we educate people in terms of the knowledge they can acquire, retain and regurgitate on demand, and we classify them as intelligent or capable according to the amount of knowledge they can regurgitate. This is a very limited definition of education, and something desperately needs to be done about it.

Another important factor in this situation is money. I have money in the sense that I own my own house—and let nobody under-rate that as a basis for self-employment. If all else fails, I can reap potatoes from my garden and sit in my house, even if it is cold, and eat them. But if you have no basic kind of capital at all, nor any basic kind of income, life is pretty difficult and it is hard not to worry about the morrow. We need to think, essentially and urgently, about giving people a guaranteed basic income in some way. And it should not be in the demeaning way that we do it at present: "If you are too idle or too ill-equipped to get yourself a job, we will support you"—for a year in this country, six months in America. We need somehow to find a way of saying to people: "You have the right to education for free in this society; you have the right to at least health-care, if not health; you have the right to at least *some* food, for free, in this society." We could at least insulate our benefits. In this country, if you are on unemployment benefit and you earn more than £2 a day venturing into self-employment (which is what everybody should do), it becomes a crime—unless you declare it. But if you declare it, it becomes a 100% marginal rate of taxation. In other words, it is deducted from your benefit. This is no way to encourage people to take care of themselves, to become self-reliant and responsible. We have a positive discrimination against self-reliance in this society.

We also need to help people to market and organise themselves, so that they aren't exploited by the large organisations. To give just one example, writers in today's society are basically ripped off, because they don't have organisations powerful enough to argue back with the big organisations. A voluntary body I am working with at the moment is putting out a volume of essays which it got from its contributors for free. Because we don't actually need the royalty, we suggested it be scrapped so the book-price could be lowered. But we discovered it would make no difference to the price of the book. So much for the value of an author's wage, or for our agents.

We need desperately to make respectable the kinds of things I was talking about earlier, the things I see as the hopeful candles for the future economic order. We need a new rhetoric. We need, for instance, to talk about *self*-employment rather than *un*employment. We need to talk about *all* forms of work as a way of contributing and creating and of giving meaning to life rather than only of jobs. We need new words for management. It is interesting that the Findhorn Foundation, in struggling with new ways of running things, has also come up with new words. As an Irishman who loves the English language I wish they had found nicer words, but I understand exactly what they *mean* by words like 'focalising' or 'attunement'. They are searching for the words to describe how you run networks, families and federal organisations.

What we need is glorious examples, because this country changes not by Napoleonic Code from the centre, but by *case-law* made respectable. We need people and organisations actually to live out the kinds of things I have been talking about, so they become fashionable. We need Findhorns—but we also need other places that do what Findhorn does in other ways: we need software companies and bakeries and breweries—ordinary run-of-the-mill organisations—to become glorious examples. We also need individuals to do this. I would like more confident, middle-class people voluntarily to leave the labour force in their 50s, so as to leave room for people coming up from below—and so that it becomes fashionable. I think it already is. I hear my middle-aged friends boasting about getting early retirement: "I say, Charles, I've got a jolly good deal out of the organisation: they're letting me go at 52 with half my pension. Isn't that absolutely super?" Ten years ago they would have hung their heads in shame and not told me. Now they boast, and I think that is a sign of a glorious example of a new rhetoric.

Finally, to pay for it all, we need some 'painter's wealth'. This country, like others in the northern hemisphere, has to earn its way by selling things that other people want but cannot make themselves. We should not abrogate unto ourselves things that other people can make. I think it is right that Margaret Thatcher has essentially exported our basic industries to the Third World, though she didn't mean to. It creates more interdependence. But we have to find something that we can do that they cannot. We need to find our painter's wealth. What I mean by 'painter's wealth' is things that depend not on the time or effort, but on the talent, skill and brains that go into them. That is the ultimate renewable resource—a funny kind of renewable resource that the more you spend of it, the bigger it grows. The more you use of your brains, knowledge and intelligence, the more you actually create in yourself.

We need in this country and in other countries to think of painter's wealth as a way of paying for the liberated and exciting society that *could* evolve. If we don't do this, poverty will drive us down the bad road that I see, to the broken-down church by the dark wood, instead of up the hill to the left in the Irishman's story.

Freedom from Work

Barrie Sherman

Barrie Sherman is a film maker, writer, lecturer and consultant who has been closely involved with the Trade Union movement in Britain. Former Director of Research at ASTMS, he is author of **The Collapse of Work**.

I have a problem—I have an awful lot to say and not much time to say it in, and I tend to speak very fast, which people don't like, so I'm caught between Scylla and Charybdis. If I were to say I'm caught between Scylla and Charybdis to most audiences in Britain, they wouldn't understand what I mean. Most people would think I was talking about a horse in the 2.30 at Haydock Park, or a Greek punk rock group. What I'm trying to say is that you are a nice, very privileged, self-selected group of people. You are self-selected because you have had the interest and initiative to come here; if I dare say it, you've also got the money to come here. An awful lot of people aren't like that, and I don't believe that people who can't come here are just the badly educated or the people who do manual work. We have a far more serious problem concerning work and leisure, and how we use and control our time, than we can just dismiss by saying, "Some people have had relatively little education and have done only manual work, therefore they can't cope with anything other than manual work." I think that's wrong.

If we look at work and why we want employment, the first thing we have to realise is that the majority of people use work to control and structure their time. People hate going to work in the morning. If we did a poll in London, Paris, Rome, New York, Washington—any major city around the world—I think we would find that no more than 5% of people would volunteer that they like travelling to work in the rush hour. People don't like the physical act of getting to work. Most people don't get much out of their job either. They don't like it; they drifted into it; there was no reason to do that particular job. So they change to a different job, but the same truths hold: they're not stretched, they don't fulfil themselves, and they don't get anywhere near realising their own potential. Yet they feel they need to work. It's like castor oil or senna-pod tea—people feel they need to take it but they hate it. There's a real dichotomy in our attitude towards work.

Work does, however, structure our day. We get up, go to work, do the things we have to do, and go home. We have a beginning, a middle and an end. If we are unemployed or retired, we tend not to take that structure with us into ordinary life. Far too many unemployed or retired people sit with a kind of writer's block in front of a blank sheet of paper and can't cope; or they experience their day as a featureless landscape. A research project in the south of London at the moment is doing pilot interviews at a Ford plant with people who have been made redundant or have retired early. They started off by interviewing the convener—the chief lay trade unionist, who is elected and represents everybody else in the plant. This particular convener had actually advised people in the past on how to cope with early retirement and how to structure their lives. He volunteered for early retirement because he wanted to get out and enjoy himself. Now, only four months after leaving his job, he starts drinking at 9.30 in the morning and the high point of his day is tea, because he sleeps through lunch. I would suggest that this is not only not unique but is also far more common than we would like to believe, and that one of our problems is that work doesn't provide people with enough flexibility and background knowledge to teach them how to cope with a non-work situation.

We are hooked on paid employment, not on work. We don't have a work ethic, we have a paid employment ethic. I can work very hard but if I am not in paid employment that ethic is not fulfilled. You can't ask a young boy or girl, "What do you want to be?" and be satisfied when they say, "I want to be a good ballroom dancer" or "I want to grow nice flowers" or "I want to be a good person". They actually have to name a paid job. We expect to hear something like 'nurse' or 'engine driver' or 'brain surgeon'. The emphasis is on paid employment, not work. This is not new; it stems from the time of the European industrial revolution and is basically a perversion of a very old work ethic. Before that time, although some towns and to some degree a mercantile society existed, the majority of people lived in an agricultural society. People didn't have to look busy in those days. That's another part of our job ethic—you have to look busy. It's no good just being at work; you can be fired if you stand there doing nothing—even if you've got nothing to do. So we all rush around like mad waving spanners or bits of paper. Before the industrial revolution, no one had to put a pitchfork over their shoulder and look busy because it was raining. They didn't feel it was necessary. They just went off into the haystack and got drunk, which was the main entertainment at the time; alcohol was the big soother. The first safety regulations at work, by the way, were actually instituted because drunk people kept falling into machines and the down time was costing too much.

So our paid employment ethic isn't really new; it is a perversion of a usefulness ethic. The work ethic used to mean being useful. It made people feel useful to others as well as to themselves. It treated work—work in a proper sense as opposed to employment—as something which was as important to other people as yourself. We don't treat work that way now. We are starting to see employment as something intrinsically good in itself, even if it no longer really fulfils a need or meets a demand. We could end up like the Marxist-based societies of Eastern Europe, where you have to believe in things like the labour theory of value: all value comes out of someone's labour. This means that if people are not working, they are not generating any economic value, the result of which is that everyone has to work. In most Moscow and Leningrad hotels, for example, there are lifts that work on the magic eye principle: as people cross the magic eye, the lift is brought to their floor. However, there is always an old lady sitting there who sees you approaching and waves a table tennis bat across the magic eye to bring the lift up or down, simply because there has to be a job created. It doesn't meet any need or demand; it's the antithesis of what work should be about; yet it is easy to make a job like that. And we also make jobs like that.

In the industrialised countries we have an unemployment problem. In the non-industrialised countries it is somewhat different because there is hidden unemployment: in conventional economic terms people have zero marginal products and are living on farms or in agricultural communities—a totally different, although nonetheless terrible, form of unemployment. In industrialised societies today there are, along with unemployment, a growing number of unmet needs. Keynes would say it is because we are not spending enough money within the economy; there is a shortfall of demands somewhere along the line. Because of this, needs in the public sector, in the health services, in the education services and in the social service field are not being met.

Let's face it, there is an infinite need for health services—and I use the word 'infinite' properly, because whilst people are mortal, we could spend the entire wealth of the world trying to keep them alive. But to be realistic about it, however, we don't even look after our old people very well, or the mentally or physically disabled. At the same time, all around the OECD there is an increase in the number of unemployed. This represents the economics of the lunatic asylum—you can't put it more bluntly than that. However, unemployment is unlikely to remain in this form, because we are moving into a wave of new technological changes which will inevitably mean we will be able to meet many of people's needs and demands far more readily, and at the same time even fewer people will need to work. I'm talking about micro-electronics of course.

Such a wave of changes isn't new. We can see a precedent for the effect of micro-electronics in the first industrial revolution. When the steam engine arrived, it was unique in two ways. Firstly, its impact was on the supply side of the economy. It helped our ancestors make and distribute things much more easily. They didn't get up and say, "Oh, it's Thursday morning, we'll go out and buy a steam engine"; it didn't add to the demand in society; it helped manufacturers and distributors to do what they did more efficiently. The second thing was that it spread everywhere. By about fifty years after it was introduced it was the motive power for every form of industry and mineral extraction and for every form of agriculture where a source of motive power other than animals was used. By then the watermills and windmills had more or less disappeared and society had moved into a steam engine phase. One of the results of this in Europe was the year of revolution in 1842, because as people moved off the land into new cities and towns the social upheavals were so massive that there were explosions everywhere. In Britain we had two utterly major political reformations to avoid the same thing happening, comparable to, say, today getting rid of parliament and replacing it with a weekly referendum using television. Political reform of that magnitude had to happen twice and Europe was hit by the deepest slump ever. People have forgotten about it. They think that the deepest slump ever occurred in the 1920s and 30s but it didn't; it happened in the 1870s to 1890s, with the result that Europeans flooded to Canada and the United States in enormous numbers, mainly because they felt there would never be jobs for them in Europe. Europe was producing more than it could demand, despite having a captive market, as it were, in all the European empires, from

51

which raw materials were sucked out and to which manufactured goods were channelled.

We are heading exactly the same way today. Micro-electronics is a supply-side technology. Who is going to go out and buy a silicon chip? Who is going to buy an integrated circuit? I once said that at a meeting and the chairman next to me opened his case and pulled out an integrated circuit he'd just bought—quite a shock! But on the whole very few people are going to buy these things. They are, however, going to use those silicon chips and those integrated circuits in machines that help increase productivity. This new technology is not even going to increase demand for other things, quite honestly, because we are *amending* products, not creating new ones for new markets. If you create a new product for a new market, you add to employment. If you create something new for an old market, you are in effect replacing a product, and if the new one is something like a digital watch you need far fewer people to make it than were needed for the old kind, so jobs disappear. And if you just amend a product, generally speaking you don't add to jobs at all. In an ecological sense micro-electronics are to be welcomed because they result in more efficient, less energy-intensive and longer-lasting products, but it also means you need fewer people to assemble them and fewer people to make the sub-assemblies. As a result of amending things we now have a motor car that can speak to us, which is very nice if you want to be spoken to by your car. I don't happen to feel that it moves the world so much further forward. We also have intelligent bathroom scales, would you believe? The whole ethos is for amendment. There are no really new products—except perhaps data bases and things like video recorders, which we wouldn't have but for micro-electronics, but their number is very limited.

The second point is that micro-electronic technology is everywhere; there are very few areas, other than some personal services, where you cannot use it. With those two distinct technical and economic characteristics of benefiting the supply side of the economy and being almost universally applicable, there hasn't been anything like micro-electronics since the introduction of the steam engine.

All across the industrialised world we find ourselves with a higher expectation factor than we had in the 19th century, when people accepted a much more basic living standard than at present. When unemployment or forced early retirement cuts people off from those expectations, it has a devastating effect on the fabric of society. We are starting to see it all around Europe in various ways, not the least being in people looking very hard for alternatives. Some alternatives are positive and constructive but some are extremely undesirable to my mind—things like glue sniffing and other drug abuse, and some of the stranger religious outpourings, although other people may not find them strange.

It is very important to work out who is likely to be at risk as a result of this new technology, and this can be done quite easily. Micro-electronics means nothing more or less than small computers. Some are dedicated, which means the programme is built in and unchangeable, such as in the speaking car. Others are programmable. A computer can in theory be programmed to do anything a person can do, providing it is a repeated action and there is no random external input. It doesn't matter whether it is a physical process, such as painting a chair or car, or welding, or whether it is doing something mental, such as assessing information for an insurance company or a bank. In theory anyone who does a job where there is a great deal of repetition can be replaced—even if that person is extremely skilled, such as a time-served, professional engineer. The fact that there may be 5,000 different functions performed by that engineer doesn't matter. It's as easy to programme 5,000 actions as it is to programme 1,000, 500, two or one.

In theory people in repetitive jobs can be replaced. But in practice the price factor comes into it. If the price of a person's labour is low, then there is less incentive to replace them. So the lowest paid, unskilled jobs—stacking shelves in supermarkets, cleaning loos, sweeping floors, all the very simple non-assembly jobs—are not replaced. Where there *is* an incentive to replace people and bring in the sophisticated machine tools is in the semi-skilled and skilled jobs. Apart from anything else it results in better quality control for the employer, so people in that middle range are always the first to go.

Then there's the management level. Most low and middle level managers take decisions based upon known parameters, so they can be replaced. But senior level managers have to deal with a great amount of external information as well. A computer can cope with a lot of information input—but if it does not have all the information, it cannot make the correct decisions. In playing chess with a computer, for example, if you restrict the information input, the computer will take decisions and beat you at the game. If you upset the chessboard, however, and put the bits back in a different order, you will find that you can win, because the computer cannot cope with that externality. It's exactly the same with some senior managers: their job is strategic planning, which includes coping with externalities, and their information input isn't rationed. Their jobs will be secure. People with imaginative and creative jobs, like accountants, writers or doctors are also secure. It's the people below them who are at risk, such as the middle managers, the people who are aides to accountants, and the medical ancillaries of this world. I would suggest that there are, at a guess, 10% who will be immune at one end because they do some form of creative job, and 10% at the other end because they will always be so badly paid it's not worth replacing them; while the people in the middle can be replaced, balancing their relative aggregate income against the cost of producing, developing, servicing and maintaining any form of system to replace them.

Industry has in many cases attempted to use robots. There is a Fiat advertisement, for example, where robots go waltzing down the floor to Italian music. Fiat wanted to fire all their welders when they introduced the robots, but the unions forced them to keep half on, which was just as well because those robots have rarely worked all at the same time. They're an absolute disaster; the design was way ahead of the technology. The reason you see them all the time on TV is, frankly, because they are a good visual gimmick. I have made TV programmes too, and my experience has been that if I show a telephone to demonstrate technology, no-one will say, "This is technological." In order to get that response I have to show a robot, because it has visual impact. But in fact the telephone holds immense implications for the way work is going to be done and where it is going to be done. The new telecommunications system combined with the proper use of word and text processors is going to decimate office employment. It's not just a question of a different kind of typewriter; there's a whole new information system developing, which means that the big commercial centres like London, New York, Paris or Rome have a real problem. You can see it happening: *where* people work is changing, as is the type of work they do and the number of people involved. The first industrial revolution got rid of the old market towns as the centres of power and influence. The current industrial revolution is going to do the same to the cities. Our office buildings in the cities will become monuments to an old industrial revolution; nobody will work in them any more and they will become a lot of large, empty dog kennels as the guard firms just patrol them.

So what can be done, and what is being done? First, you have to have financial security. I work in national politics, and I believe that financial security has to come from that national level. It has to come about through something like a negative income tax, which I think is a flexible solution. We have the technology to introduce it now, because we have just computerised the Inland Revenue, which has cost about 30,000 jobs. Negative income tax isn't a raving left-wing argument, by the way; it was invented by Milton Friedman, *the* capitalist economist. As a concept it is simplicity itself. A threshold income, say £100 per week for a single person, is agreed. Everyone going above this pays tax; below it, they receive money. Family and personal circumstances are compensated for by a normal code number. The system replaces welfare, unemployment and pension payments and extends F.I.S. considerably. It is the prerequisite for doing anything else. If the nation and its people are not financially secure, government cannot expect any person, family or unit to fulfil their potential.

I agree wholeheartedly that solutions have to be community-based, but I think you also have to define communities and realise that they shift and change. Externalities always intervene; communities change and die in the same way organisations do, so it isn't very easy to make a fixed point of them. However, within those communities what we have to do is try to redefine employment into work. One of the things I suggest is that we talk in terms of free time and tithed time—time used for service to others, whether paid or unpaid (and if you are financially secure, it doesn't really matter). This gets us back to pre-industrial revolution ethics as opposed to today's industrial revolution ethics. The other thing about working in the community-based context is that no-one really knows yet what popular planning is. I have made five films about the Greater London Enterprise Board, the people who helped with an experiment in popular planning in the London Borough of Newham, and it isn't working terribly well. It's a marvellous idea but no-one has thought it through yet. No-one really knows what socially useful products are. Until we do, and until we work out when and how we should make them and the priorities involved, we're a little bit lost and floundering. I would argue very strongly that we need a new framework to start from. It's very easy to say we need a new framework, of course, but exceptionally difficult to put into practice.

We have to make secondary employment—things like contract-only labour—respectable. A lot of people are doing it because there's nothing else for them to do. It's fine if it's truly voluntary. It's not fine if it's just cheap labour, and right now it is just cheap labour. There's a lot of money to play with. Roughly £14 billion a year are spent in Britain on keeping people unemployed and doing nothing. There is an equivalent sum in France, in West Germany and, would you believe, in Japan, because Japan also is now starting to have a large unemployment problem, including a hidden one, because people are being compulsorily retired at 50 after being kept on for two or three years doing nothing.

Finally in terms of what to do, I think there has to be a change in the education system. Firstly, instead of teaching people how to pass exams, we should teach them how to learn. It doesn't matter whether we have an examination system or not; it is the ability to learn which is important, given all the changes we have to cope with today. We have to confront life day by day and, without being able to learn, we can't do it. Teaching people to learn means we must have a different system of teaching. It is not necessarily the subjects that are wrong at present; it's the way they are taught. All subjects should be taught as a method of learning that subject and also as a method of learning about learning. Teachers I have talked to in Britain and the States tell me this is the theory they work on, but they patently don't put the theory into practice. I'm suggesting that the theory *does* go into practice. Secondly, our whole education system in Britain is dictated by the universities. However, only 10% of people ever go to university, so 90% are learning a lot of stuff they needn't really bother with. It's no use to them at any time, now or in the future, especially if they are not learning to learn from it. Thirdly, we make education available almost only to young people up to the age of 18 or 22. It should be constantly available as a consumer resource, so that people can dip in and out of it whenever they wish, right up to the age of 90 or 100. It should be possible to tap into it like the water or electricity supply. I'm not trying to devalue education, but I would like to demystify it. Education should be a national utility for all, and not necessarily just for training people for jobs, because vocational teaching at a time of rapid technological change has to be almost as lunatic as unemployment at a time of rising need. Education needs these sorts of changes. There isn't, in my opinion, a more conservative establishment in Britain than the teaching profession, and that means the changes are going to be hard and long.

Above all, we need to amend the work ethic. We can't just move into a leisure ethic, otherwise all the people who are working are going to say, "Why me?"—and quite rightly too. We need to amend the work ethic into a usefulness ethic, and that has to come about through education. By nature it will be a slow change. I am literally talking about a hiatus—a nasty, rather worrying period of a minimum of 25 to 30 years—when many transitions will take place and when with the best will in the world we are going to be as uncomfortable as hell. There is an old Haitian proverb which I think should be our watchword through this period and it goes as follows: "If work were a good thing, the rich would have found a way of keeping it all to themselves."

Is Democracy Possible at Work?

Ian Gordon-Brown

Ian Gordon-Brown has worked for many years in the field of industrial and organisational psychology, including the area of worker participation. He is joint Founder and Director of the Centre for Transpersonal Psychology in London and is a leading authority on ways of expanding consciousness.

Will democracy work in an industrial setting? Will it work in schools, hospitals or within the bureaucracies of our state? From what I have seen since I came into the organisational world in 1949 as an industrial psychologist, I would say that the answer is "Yes, but it's very difficult." We live in a complex and untidy world and democracy comes and goes. As a psychologist I am obviously going to talk about the psychological side. But I am also going to talk about the nitty-gritty stuff, because one of my love affairs has been with the world of manufacturing industry where, it seems to me, 'the real people' live.

The Unconscious Factor

Not so long ago I was talking to someone who had recently qualified as a Jungian analyst. I had known him in the business and industrial world too. He was saying, "You know, it's absolutely fascinating: Jungians are concerned with love and oneness and helping people grow, but the power struggle that's going on in my particular neck of the woods has to be experienced to be believed. How different from industry, where if somebody's on a power trip we all know about it and pull his or her leg—usually *his* leg." "Yes," I said, "and I wonder what the unconscious factor is in industry"—because, of course, power was the unconscious factor in that Jungian group and the conscious factor in industrial groups—"I wonder if it's love?" And both of us agreed that at the unconscious level love was a very powerful motivating factor in industry as we had known it.

I have worked in the world of voluntary organisations as well as in that of industrial and commercial ones, and believe I have experienced more love in the industrial world than ever in any voluntary organisation. People in industry may not know about the things that are recognised at places like the Findhorn Foundation but there's a lot of good, earthy human reality around in business and the world of work.

Mass, individual and group consciousness

Unconscious factors are central then to the question of whether a democracy can work in organisations. An organisation, and for that matter an individual, can be likened to an iceberg. Sixth-sevenths is below the surface; it is in the unconscious. Most people at work live in the unconscious part of their organisation, they don't actually know what is going on: generally speaking they don't know about policy, they don't know what the long term forward plan is, and often they don't even know what is happening in the department next door. Usually only a small number of people are conscious both as individuals and organisationally, and many do not really want to know, at least until some crisis comes along which affects them personally. It seems to me that this is why large organisations used once to work, at least after a fashion. The majority of people did not want to know, so the few who did had power, whether they were managers or worker representatives.

But this is changing. More and more people are unwilling and unable to be organisationally unconscious while growing as individuals. They are emerging assertively from the mass. This is the real reason why size is such a central question and why large organisations, at least in the form we have known them, are doomed.

But the emergence of individuals from the mass is not enough. It is only one stage in the process. True democracy can only come with the development of group consciousness, where individuals can speak their minds and express their feelings, perhaps against the current of group energy, while remaining within the group as fully accepted and accepting members.

So our experiments in democracy—and I would bet that Findhorn is no exception—are imperfect, untidy and full of problems. This is only to be expected. All organisations are a mixture of mass, individual and group consciousness and most of us have a long way to go before we reach a balance where democracy will really work.

Factors for Success

What conditions need to be satisfied if participation and democracy are to work in organisations? The central factor, I believe, has to do with leadership, often the charisma and energy of one or two specially creative individuals. I remember listening to Ernest Bader speak at the opening conference of what later became the Common Ownership Movement. He was outlining his ideas and principles. Very impressive and high sounding. Then at question time a woman got up and said, "I'm his personnel officer. Don't pay too much attention to Ernest's ideas. Most of us who work for the firm are not really interested in them. But we work for him and do what he wants because we love him." There's the theme of love again. If the boss is the right sort employees may say, "He or she's a bastard," but they say it affectionately and admiringly—in their guts they recognise the genuine quality of the person.

Let me take another quote to illustrate my theme. A. Connor Wilson, founder of Airflow Developments Ltd, which became a common ownership company in 1973, states: "A common ownership structure, of itself, does not create harmony—it only provides a sort of framework in which harmony is more likely to be achieved. For one thing people (at Airflow) know that monetary benefits can only be produced by their own cooperative effort, and even then they may have different ideas about how the benefits are to be shared out. We still have to run a company with a mixture of ordinary human beings. We still run up against personal jealousies and personality conflicts. At a general meeting of the community only about one third of the members turn up and if you ask some of them what our common ownership structure means to them, they may make a very noncommittal reply."

International Comparisons
There was some interesting research done by the International Institute for Labour Studies, an offshoot of ILO, in the early 1970s. This research investigated the factors that made for success in industrial democracy and worker participation in management. The study covered France, West Germany, India, Israel, Japan, Poland, Spain, UK, USA and Yugoslavia. We should note that there was some communist representation. The report states: "One conclusion stands out above all others. The only factor common to every study of successful participation in all ten countries was management attitudes." That is, the quality, feeling, style, openness, honesty, integrity and so forth of the top people. "This was as true in socialist Poland and Yugoslavia as

in free-enterprise USA and held good for all the other countries too. None of the other factors was of the same order of importance or so universally applicable."

This is a fundamental truth, it seems to me. In my experience, when democracy works it is usually because there are a few people in key positions who are absolutely pivotal. It may be the convener of shop stewards, by the way; it doesn't have to be the chief executive.

Growth by Splitting
I don't want to confine myself to talking about industrial organisations. There are some very interesting examples of group process in the world of the esoteric and of voluntary organisations. I think that organisations on the whole—and there are interesting exceptions, of which Findhorn is one—are at what I would call the amoeba stage of development: they grow by splitting. It is fascinating to see what happens upon the death of the founder or the charismatic initiator of an organisation—be it a company, a movement, a church or whatever. Within five years, if not earlier, there is almost certainly a split. Even if they do manage to hold it together, there's usually a split going on underneath. I once said to the late John Davy of the anthroposophical movement, "It seems to me that the Steiner people are the only exception to this rule in our modern world." He replied, "If only you knew the inside story!"

When a split occurs it is frequently along ideological lines. There are those who say, "We must continue to be true to the teaching of the founder." And there are others who say, "If the founders were here to-day, they wouldn't be so silly as to do that." It happens in business as well. I have been involved in a number of splits and they no longer worry me. They all seem to have produced useful results. They had to happen. A split is like a scattering of the seed. It is a kind of reproduction or procreation and releases a lot of creativity. But there is also a lot of unnecessary fighting, and I believe that in building the organisations of the future we have to create much looser structures so that democratic involvement and participative processes can have room to grow creatively and without the infighting and blocked energies so common today.

Life Cycles of Organisations and Ideas
Changes happen not only when the founding father or mother dies. Organisations have life cycles; they are like people. They are born; they go into adolescence; there's a stage when they are the young hero and

everything runs well for them, including their love affair with the market place; then they enter middle age and something happens and they begin to die. It is actually necessary that organisations die. There are far too many voluntary organisations, for example, which do no useful work but are kept alive by endowments. Just as we sometimes keep people alive too long by the nonsenses of medical science, so we keep a lot of organisations going when they should have been wound up long before.

While it is people who matter most in the functioning of organisations, we need also to look at the life cycle of ideas. Can you guess when the following piece was written? "We have taken in hand no small task. We aim at being the voice of those societies which are building up the industrial system of the future upon the basis of direct representative self-government. Not a delusive self-government, so unwieldy, so indirect, so machine-like, so centralised, that the individual worker feels himself completely lost and helpless; but a real and practical self-government in which each shall have a real and effective voice in controlling the industry in which he spends his days. We aim at a system in which men will feel a real and direct connection between the vigour, the care and the intelligence they use, and the reward which comes to themselves and their fellow-workers. Not certainly at a system in which a man shall work for his own family alone, but one which shall indentify his interest with the interest of the community of fellow-workers of whom he is one. Lastly, we aim at a system in which these communities of workers shall in their turn ally themselves together for the common good. In plain language, we aim at being the organ of the co-partnership movement in this country ...." That was written in August 1894 and published in Vol. 1, No. 1 of the *Labour Co-Partnership Journal*, the publication of an organisation originally called the Labour Association for Promoting Cooperative Production Based on the Co-Partnership of the Workers (what a mouthful) which was founded in 1884 and continues today as the Industrial Participation Association. If it was not for touches of unfamiliar language it would be easy to believe it had been written today. We are seeing the re-emergence of themes like love, cooperation and democracy in industry. It is a cyclic re-emergence of ideas and impulses that have been around before and we do a disservice to ourselves and to others if we do not recognise this historical ebb and flow. We are seeing it again through, for example, the 5th Directive of the EEC that states the desirability of having workers on the boards of companies.

The Size of Organisations

The question of size seems to be as critical as the right kind of leadership. During the 1970s I spent a lot of time going up and down the country organising conferences and seminars on the theme of industrial democracy and worker participation. Those involved were managers at every level and trade union representatives and officials. One constant theme emerged: everybody would be talking about how difficult industrial democracy was until somebody said, "Well, we don't have any of these problems, but of course we're small." When you asked *how small*, it was never more than 500 people.

There is a universal recognition now of the importance of size—and not just among small companies. I remember talking with the managing director of Royal Dutch Shell about nine years ago, because I had picked up his comment on the size question in the *Journal of International Management*. He said, "The big organisations are like the dinosaurs of the past era. There is no future for them. We can go quite a long way to arrange our business so that it's a lot of small organisations linked together, but it's still not going to work." I think he's right. Somehow or other the size issue is critical. I once went along to talk to a firm that Ernest Bader sponsored. There were three people working in a couple of rooms developing a boat-making business. I heard later that the business had gone well, that they had expanded to fill the building they were in and had a chance to move to another building down the road. Filling the building they were in meant that there were 25 people in the company, and going down the road meant that they could go up to 75—and there was certainly enough business for that. But the group decided not to move. The reason was interesting: they said, "If we move, we are not going to know everybody in the business equally well." For them, 20 to 25 was the critical size factor, and their priority was to stay small. I once talked with another person from a big oil company that had decided wherever possible not to allow any units of the company to grow beyond 200 people. When I asked why, he said, "That's the largest unit that any one person is capable of looking after successfully."

You can play around with the figures any way you like, but it seems to me that the size question is one of the central factors in the functioning of organisations.

Practical Steps

A great many businesses—manufacturing and retail, large and small, charitable and profit making—have experimented with ways of making participation work. When I was Director of the Industrial Participation Association we started a series of conferences at which joint management-worker teams talked about what they were doing to develop democracy in industry. It was fascinating to see the wide range of different practices that people had tried and the creativity and imagination that had been used to make them work.

When I entered the industrial world joint consultation was all the vogue, to be followed by communications and company newspapers. There are fashions in these matters: new ideas which are in reality old ideas come and go, each lasting a few years and then giving way to the next. I suspect this is because particular devices and techniques never work on their own. Indeed the practical arrangements must always be subservient to the spirit if they are to work. But let me comment briefly on some of the more enduring ways.

Profit sharing and employee shareholding, as well as common and cooperative ownership, have a long history and there are companies that have managed to continue with such schemes for well over half a century. Consultation and shared decision making in many forms also endure. Collective bargaining between representatives of management and the trades unions is by far the most widely practised arrangement. But elective company councils in many different forms, often alongside collective bargaining arrangements, are common. I note that they only really work when given real power to influence decision making and to make decisions that count in the lives of those who work in the enterprise. Indeed, consultation without power to affect decisions of moment is now widely regarded as phoney.

Communication is another enduring issue. All the devices of the media are practised: company newspapers, tannoy and internal television, information meetings, notice boards, the lot. And because people in business are amateur communicators, their best will often just produce boredom! Most of us don't actually want to know everything all the time and are content to let the eager beavers get on with it, provided we can trust them. So the best companies move to open information systems, where there are no secrets, except the personal files of individual employees.

One of the most interesting developments of recent years is annual general meetings for employees. Some chief executives spend several weeks visiting different sites, holding a series of meetings at each, where anything goes and no holds are barred. Once you start you have to continue! This is the principle that there is nothing like the horse's mouth.

A lot of jobs are routine and boring, so experiments have been made to enrich jobs and give responsibility back to people on the shop floor, the coal face, the counter. And at the other end of the scale workforce representatives begin from time to time to sit on company boards; in some countries the law requires this.

But it is hard work and I have met many who have worked their hearts out for years and then say, "It's too much, we are back where we started; I must get out." Those who try to push the democratic impulse forward can come up against tremendous and soul-destroying inertia. Let us remember that there is this dark face as we face our bright new age morning sun and be charitable to those who try but fail and become disillusioned. The French are right when they say "Plus ca change, mais c'est toujours la même chose."

Masculine and Feminine in Organisations

I speak from the perspective that masculine and feminine energies are found in most forms of life. Feminine energies are to be found in men as well as women and masculine energies in women as well as men. Both exist in organisations. When either is suppressed or blocked there is trouble. For the past 2000 or more years, at least in the occident, masculine energies have seemed to dominate at the conscious level and the feminine dimensions of the psyche have been pushed underground, into the individual and collective unconscious. One of the most important events of our time is that the feminine is surfacing into consciousness. The signs of this are present everywhere, and the implications are quite literally earth-shattering. Please note that I am aware of the problems of language and stereotyping but do not have time to deal with them here. Note also that I am talking about masculine and feminine *energies*.

If you look at successful organisations you will find, I think invariably, that the feminine has found space to be present. It is not suppressed. The charismatic founders of successful movements and organisations embody both masculine and feminine energies within themselves. That is why they appeal to both heart and head. Charisma or magnetism, however you define it, reflects a coming together of masculine and feminine, sometimes indeed an inner marriage.

You will not find many representatives of the feminine principle in senior positions in the organisational hierarchy. But they will be present elsewhere—a secretary, a tea lady, the porter or caretaker. You will also find them dotted around in areas of towns that have managed to retain that special quality or atmosphere we associate more with villages. Again their position may be humble, as postman, milkman, street cleaner, the woman who runs the corner shop. Barbara Somers and I have come to call such people 'Ents', after the tree spirits in Tolkien, because when we lived in South Kensington our postman was an Ent; he was a lovely man and like a walking tree. While these people are present they preserve that mysterious and magical balance of the feminine and masculine. But if the masculine starts to push through some ruthless and unnecessary re-organisation, the 'Ents' will usually go away. The same happens with certain forms of redevelopment in towns—Ents can't live by six-lane highways.

I can do no more here than say that true democracy is not just about 'the arrangements or structures or techniques', important though these are. It is also about feeling, atmosphere, heart and flow—the spaces in between. We need agendas, rules and regulations, competence and order. We also need spontaneity, intuition, flow and that random quality that evokes beauty and genius in the everyday. The masculine without the feminine makes a sorry mess of organisations of all kinds. The feminine without the masculine is no better, just different.

Archetypes

Finally let me say a few words about one of the new frontiers of this subject. It arises from the fact that as people we are not all made of the same stuff. The same goes for organisations. There are fundamental qualitative differences, archetypal imprints if you like, that we ignore at our peril, for they determine a whole range of things: organisational style, methods of work, values and goals, the people we can work with and so on.

When we started the Centre for Transpersonal Psychology we felt that we came under the archetype of the priest-healer and teacher of consciousness (to be distinguished from the teacher of facts and theories, a quite different archetypal imprint). Now the priest-healer/ consciousness teacher works essentially through radiation and magnetism. Advertising, marketing, building up mailing lists—the promotional techniques that are so rightly a part of the business world—are alien to this archetype. Indeed I believe they are counter-productive in the longer run. So we decided that we would have literature, but not advertise, and that instead of regularly mailing our programme, we would require people to write in and ask! We said to ourselves, "If we are any good, and if we are magnetic, those whom we can help will hear of us." And so it has proved to be. It has worked very well and, purely at the business level, we are one of the most successful operations in our field. Being true to your archetype, which is another way of being true to yourself, is a recipe for success as well as fulfilment.

Let me give a few individual examples, and then come back to organisations. People are constantly being promoted out of their archetype, or sometimes indeed into it. So the good tradesman becomes the bad foreman; the fulfilled scientist an unhappy administrator; the less than competent manager an excellent consultant and so on. Equally in the mid-life crisis people often change their 'archetypal affiliation'. For we all have the imprint of several archetypes within us, and the imprint of our personal centre which may be dominant in the first half of life may be quite different from the stuff of which our Soul, the Self, is made, and it is to this that many of us move in the second half of life. So the creative mid-life career change will often move us closer to our essence. One of my personal battles has been between the king/ruler/power archetype, which drew me to politics, and the priest/healer energy which pushed me to my present profession. In my earlier years it was not clear which was primary and which was secondary. I think many of us face this sort of problem. Now my king is quite happy to run the Centre according to the rules laid down by the priest/healer!

At the collective level it seems to me difficult to account for the last 2000 years in terms of Pisces. But during this period the archetype of the idealist, the devotee whose 'God' is perfection, has also ruled. This is another reason why splits so often turn into ideological battles. However, this archetype seems to be withdrawing into the unconscious and that of the magician is surfacing. The magician represents a quite different energy. Manifestation is one of his or her keynotes. Network organisation is very much an expression of the energy of the magician. This archetypal shift, as we transit from Pisces to Aquarius, is one of the fundamental conditioning factors of our time.

Now I am not arguing for specialisation. Most organisations need a fair representation of different archetypal energies. Each will need its rulers, managers, consultants, planners, teachers, researchers, technicians, mechanics, builders, craftsmen and so on, and we should be lost without a few recording angels.

What I *am* advocating is that we become more conscious of the kind of organisation of which we are a part, of its fundamental energy and archetypal imprint and, indeed, the different energies of its parts. Then we can help that archetype, which is in one sense the soul of the organisation, to work according to its true nature. Then purpose, style, modes of work, values, the shape of the organisation and the rhythm of its life can come harmoniously together and, with a bit of luck, which we all need, success and fulfilment will follow.

Business in Society: The New Initiative

Francis Kinsman

Francis Kinsman is a freelance management consultant and Co-Founder of the London-based Business Network, a forum for exploring the human factor in business. He is author of **The New Agenda**, *a comprehensive guide to our profoundly changing social environment.*

For the past twelve years I've been a futurist. What this entails is talking to my clients, who are generally large organisations, about the political, economic, technological, social and increasingly also now the spiritual changes that are beginning to take place. I try to help them ride these changes like a surfer rides the waves—not controlling change but recognising that they do have options in response to it—so that thus they have the power to create their own futures rather than just blundering on into them regardless.

Being a Virgoan with Libra in the ascendant, the other thing I tend to do is to feed my own naive compulsion to build beautiful neat bridges between impossible opposites—like love and business in this instance. It may sound totally incongruous, but it is just beginning to dawn on business people that it is profitable to love thy neighbour, which means that at any minute now there are going to be an awful lot of happy neighbours about. Let me give you some examples.

Ten years ago a friend of mine who was the manager of Shell in a developing country held a meeting with some of his colleagues on the public affairs stance that Shell should adopt towards the people of this country. At one point, he took a deep breath and said, "I think we should love them more." There was the most appalling scene, shouting, purple-faced people thumping the table, white-faced people wishing the ground would open up and swallow them ... but a few others whispering, "Thank God, someone has said it at last." That was ten years ago.

Seven years ago, National Westminster Bank was faced with an urgent staff problem, caused by having too many 50-year-old managers and assistant managers, which meant tremendous competition for jobs at that level and just below it, and a consequent sag in morale due to diminishing promotion opportunities. But rather than make them redundant, the National Westminster Bank came up with an ingenious plan. They created a subsidiary company called National Westminster Enterprises and transferred 200 of these people into it. They were given the same salary with the same increments, the same fringe benefits, the same pension, the same holiday and sick rights, everything. They were essentially in the same organisation, but this bit of it was very different. It was not only non-profit-making but it was loss-making, because it paid the salaries of these people and made them available as a free human resource to voluntary organisations, at the choice of the individuals concerned.

Naturally, when the voluntary organisations heard about it hundreds of them wrote in. "Please lend us our own private bank manager ... to reorganise our accounts department ... to help set up this new unit here ... to sort out the administrative mess we've got into there ...." So every one of these transformed managers had a dozen alternatives to choose from. They suddenly found themselves not in a competitive, aggro, macho job where they had to assert themselves and push and shove and do all the things that they really didn't want to do at all, but in a job where they were fulfilled, needed and had made their own choice of exactly what they wanted to do. At last they were *people* rather than miserable automata. They were delighted, their wives were delighted, the charities were delighted too, naturally enough. Everybody was delighted, but the National Westminster Bank was slightly embarrassed as well, and didn't want too much made of it. That was seven years ago.

Then, two years ago, I interviewed the Chairman of ICI, John Harvey-Jones, in the course of which he said two things which in combination were stunningly paradoxical. First he said, "ICI has 66,000 employees in the UK; by the year 2015 I reckon there will be 3,000 full-time employees and a hell of a lot of part-timers." Then he said, "We must love our employees more." An amazing statement, in any language, from the Chairman of ICI. That was two years ago.

Margaret Thatcher recently remarked, "If only every company in the country was run like Marks and Spencer, it would be a very different country." Too right. Because Marks and Spencer, besides being an extraordinarily successful organisation, has an employee relations policy and a consumer relations policy famous throughout the country, even the world, perhaps. Their relationship with all their stakeholders is as good as they can make it—and that is *why* they are successful.

A couple of months ago, it was their 100th birthday. They didn't have a cocktail party to celebrate, they started a fund-raising scheme instead. They provided charitable money for each of their 260 stores to distribute within their neighbourhoods—£2 million in the aggregate— to be matched pound for pound by fund-raising activities amongst the employees, who then decided locally to what causes that money should be donated. So all over the country you will now find Marks and Spencer helping all kinds of local initiatives, in small different individualistic ways—some concerned with the unemployed, some with the arts, some with minority groups, some with disabled people and so forth. This is not M & S at board level saying, "Right, I think we'll give Oxfam £250,000 this year." It is the choice of their people locally, in a person-to-person exchange, based on their recognition that People Matter Most. So that was two months ago.

Now we come to last week, when the head of the biggest supermarket chain in France, Edouard La Claire, announced that for the winter his shops would give away food to anybody who asked for it. The cynical French press remarked that those to whom he gave it away would have pinched it anyway, so he wasn't actually losing anything. But you see what is happening. The recipients of this love—because that's what it is, and let's come out into the open and name it—are happy, the staff are happy, the public are happy, everybody is happy. There is a multiplier effect here about all these stories, and they are cropping up more and more frequently too. Something else is going on.

Now, a cynic would say that a lot of all this was manipulative, politically inspired, mere tokenism, and at best only a drop in the ocean anyway. I'll go part of the way with that analysis, because there is much here—not necessarily in the examples I've given but in the general flow of it—which is cynically performed to keep the natives happy and stop them getting restless. And perhaps it doesn't seem much of an effort when you compare it to the kind of profits these companies are making. In the United States there is an organisation called the Two Percent Club, a group of companies which dedicate themselves to donating two percent of their profits per year to good causes. The club has quite a large number of members, whereas here in Britain there is a very small membership of a *One* Percent Club, so we have a long way to go. But in essence, I believe it is less of a drop in the ocean than a straw in the wind, and the wind is getting up. We are approaching an experience which is going to be very, very different—a global economic crisis of awesome magnitude. Something else indeed is going on.

As I see it, we are now in earthquake country. Like animals before an earthquake, more and more of us sense something, without quite knowing what it is—but it makes people nervous, irritable and oddly behaved. They are restive, the hair is crawling up the back of their spines as growing numbers of them detect these first rumbles deep down. Society is rapidly dividing into two camps—those who know and those who don't want to know—and, by the time it happens for real, nobody will be able to say "I didn't know."

Now of course those who don't want to know are exactly the people who are ostensibly keeping control over everything—and actually ensuring that things are going to get worse by so doing. Because, going back to the geological analogy, we are in for shock rather than creep. Geological creep is when the Earth's tectonic plates push up against each other infinitely slowly and after about 40 million years there are the Himalayas. What is about to happen in the San Andreas Fault, and metaphorically speaking to us, is geological shock. In parts of the structure there is total resistance to change so that, having not moved an inch for 130 years, any day now this thing is going to rip the earth apart.

The diehards have a vested interest in the status quo, so they are trying to keep everything nice and tidy and exactly the same. King Canute in modern dress. They still outnumber what you might call the sensitives who know, but the sensitives are on the up and up, particularly among those who guide the country's largest enterprises. If you think about it, those people have got to the top because they have that flair for knowing what's going to happen next, that intuitive feel for what it is going to take to survive. So, with this in mind, I went and talked to thirty of them about it, the result of which was a book I wrote, *The New Agenda*. I started each of these interviews by asking a single question: "What are the social factors that are going to have the biggest impact on British management between now and 1990?" The wonderful thing is that you can write the answer on the back of a postage stamp: it is the message that 'People Matter Most', in whatever capacity you like, as employees, consumers, pensioners, suppliers, the public at large, everyone with whom the organisation has contact. As long as an organisation has that at its heart, as its philosophy, then it will survive. Without it, it has no chance. It may succeed in the short term, but in the long run it will inevitably run into trouble.

When I came out of some of these interviews, I found myself really moved by what people had said and by how marvellously they had opened up to me. So I got very excited and we arranged a great dinner party for 14 of them, in the hope that when they got together they would create something that would move mountains. What I failed to realise was they wouldn't open up to each other at all. These enormously influential men were terrified of admitting to their peers the things they had said to me confidentially; they were absolutely not going to reveal the warmth of their thoughts, their feelings and their hearts to each other. Then I'm afraid I got very frustrated and angry, because only I knew what was there inside them all the time. So I said, "Look, there is supposed to be something magnificent coming out of this and you're giving me nothing. Where is it?" But even that didn't shake them; they just said "Oh, have another port." So I did and to hell with it.

Things weren't going to work that way, then, but yet the treasure was all there, waiting to be uncovered. There had to be a different approach, and a clue to its nature came through the Business Network. This is an organisation started by Edward Posey and myself two years ago—what you might call a refuge for battered business people. It's a forum where people can talk about business together in terms which are not necessarily just about profit; believing that there is more in business than simply that, but being afraid to say so in front of their working colleagues in case it gets onto their personnel record. It's actually quite dangerous saying this kind of thing in a big organisation—you can get shunted off to a Siberian power-station for the rest of your career—but still people have this deep need to say it. For example, going back to John Harvey-Jones, a man of immense power, when I told him that many of his sentiments were echoed among his fellow interviewees, he said, "Do you mean to say there are other nutters like me out there?" This is the feeling so many business people have. They don't actually believe that everybody else has the same fears and hopes and desperate longings to get it right on a personal basis.

The Business Network is an association that provides a space for people to share, to compare and to voice their beliefs and concerns about this. But at the same time it is strictly a club; fun, but it fulfils no more than an informal function. Edward and I concluded that there was a commercial need here as well, a market in other words, for a business service. Together with Liz Hosken, who had joined us in the Business Network, we formed a consultancy called New Initiative, the purpose of which is to enhance the human dimension in management and to act as a positive catalyst in the equation of change.

The first thing we did was to put on a seminar at the London Business School, a legit venue if ever there was one. If you have a seminar at the London Business School, people assume there's going to be nothing too long-haired and flaky about it. We have to be subtle that way, to conjure up the element of magic in the juxtaposition of the traditional and the wild. That was the 'ingredient X' of the seminar—shocking people into thinking everyday business things all over again from the beginning, by juxtaposing these opposites and then building bridges between them. *PUT YOURSELF INTO THE POSITION OF OUR ELECT OFFICIALS*

The subject matter for the day was our current employment/unemployment crisis. We had John Harvey-Jones talking about the changing relationship between employees and organisations, Sir Peter Parker talking about the need for business to come to terms with the whole basic fact of unemployment, and Professor Charles Handy talking about future work patterns. It was an absolutely blue-chip line-up. But at the same time—and this is where Liz Hosken plays such a vital role—we also introduced these magic feminine touches, stimulating the right-hand side of the brain as well as the left. So on the day, this rather stark lecture-hall was full of flowers and we had Pachelbel's Canon playing in the background. All these upright businessmen marched in having absorbed their coffee and their traditionalist chit-chat with each other, and suddenly there were flowers and music everywhere, and they sat down very nervously indeed.

But worse was to come, because Liz came to the front to welcome them and said, "In New Initiative we generally like to start with a quiet moment to dismiss all the surface cares and worries, so that we can really focus on what we have to think about, so I suggest you close your eyes and breathe." This really freaked them out. Some couldn't take it at all. But others were caught off guard and got hooked—like one of the senior training managers of Shell who went back to his office after the day's experience, called in the colleague who had introduced him to us and said, "Richard, look, I cannot understand what happened yesterday. There was John Harvey-Jones, surrounded by flowers, breathing. Who are these people? Get them in to lunch with us for heaven's sake. I want to find out what's going on."

74

What is going on is that something else is going on—the telephone has hardly stopped ringing ever since. Business people are half drawn and half threatened by this combination of the square and the oddball. I come from a fairly traditional background, so I can put my stiff white collar on and become a mole in the establishment. I can get the old hat people in, because they think "Oh, good old Francis, we all know him—he's a bit of a weirdo but I expect it'll be all right." But once they're in, Edward waves his beard about and Liz totally unnerves them with her Leonine power and suddenly they don't know what on earth is happening to them. In actual fact, we have them on toast.

So what do we actually do with them? Well, we are working with these business people at several levels—one to one, almost as counsellors; with small groups of 20 to 30; as creative consultants within large organisations; and generally drawing up the fundamental blueprints for the different business and economic facets of a new kind of society. In particular we are very much involved with community groups, and are introducing the idea of self-help and individual empowerment into the thinking of the business world, so that both these two sides realise they can help each other to their own enormous mutual advantage.

With the groups of 20 to 30, we are developing something we call the Future Now Programme, which positively explores the fact that the crises of individuals, of their organisations and of society itself are all human crises, and as such all contain the elements of both opportunity and danger. The solutions of these crises as it were echo each other harmonically up and down the third, the fifth and the octave notes of this human key, so that what is relevant in one sphere has its application in another.

To put it a different way, everything conforms to a sort of genetic pattern—it is like a hologram, where, if it is broken, every single piece reproduces the original picture. The human body is composed of cells, each of which has the same chromosome pattern in its nucleus, but any individual cell may be part of an eyeball or a liver or a kneecap. The cells with the same chromosome pattern attract each other in a mysterious way, so that you end up with a network of kindred interests, a body of opinion, you might say, though the metaphor is now getting a bit stretched. It is something to do with the fact that there is a sort of cosmic glue that helps bind everything together that wants to be bound together.

The three of us are an example. Liz and Edward and I decided to suss out whether we would like to work together on a commercial basis. We went away to the South of France to have a brainstorm together about it, because there's no better place to have a brainstorm than the South of France. There was a moment when we all said, "Right, yes, we've got it. This is what we're going to do together." After that everything moved very quickly. When we got back to England, we asked an astrologer friend of ours to do a chart of that moment, and amongst other things he said, "This is very extraordinary, because this creature you have created is to you, Edward, your child; and to you, Liz, it's your father, but a father who truly listens to the wisdom of his daughter; and to you, Francis, it's your wife."

We believe there is a living to be made by ensuring that love and business really do come together as a transformative force throughout our society. The cynic might respond that in that case we're in for a long diet of locusts and wild honey. But I don't feel that at all. I feel something else is indeed going on and that there *is* a new initiative—not just our bit of it, but a genuine recognition that the People-Matter-Most bandwagon is on the move. So let's go for it.

Part III

The New Local Economic Order

The New Local Economic Order

Guy Dauncey

Guy Dauncey is a freelance writer and broadcaster who focuses on the transformative potential within the unemployment crisis. He edits a newsletter for the British Unemployment Resource Network and is author of **The Unemployment Handbook** *and* **Nice Work if You Can Get It**. *The following chapter, based on his talk at the* **New Economic Agenda** *conference, was written specially for this book.*

DEPRECIATING
DEVALUATING
DECLINING
CURRENCY

"Even a local economy needs people to love it."

Something is astir in the land of economics. The territory which has for so long been 'the dismal science' is showing signs that it is about to undergo a powerful transformation. For far too long much of economics has been the study of who could get the most from whom, and at what price. Such issues as beauty, human fulfilment or higher purpose have been generally absent. No wonder it has felt so dry and dead. It has been dealing only with the bones, the heart and soul having long fled.

In small communities, cities and towns all over Britain, and in many other countries, people are now asking new questions about their local economies and are then seeking new answers in practical ways. They are being prompted by problems of unemployment, poverty or a feeling of lack of control over their local economies. They are experimenting with new agencies to assist people to set up their own businesses and cooperatives; they are establishing businesses which are owned and controlled by local people, called 'community businesses'; they are setting up schemes to give special help to young people to start up their own businesses; they are conducting community appraisal studies and popular planning exercises to encourage local people to think ahead about their local area and its economy, so that there can be a new vision of what is possible and a basis for action; they are purchasing old abandoned factories or warehouses and converting them into community-owned business/sports/training/social centres; they are seeking ways to set up local financial institutions, so that local money can be channelled to support local development; they are establishing close relationships with nearby colleges, so that the skills and expertise of students and staff can be made available to assist local businesses with such matters as product development; they are developing local energy policies, so that towns and cities do not have to earn large sums of money simply to buy in unnecessary supplies of oil, coal and electricity—and so it goes on.[1] From such tiny shoots as these, a new landscape is appearing.

'The New International Economic Order' is a dream which was unveiled to the world in the early 1970s at the time of the Brandt Commission into world poverty, hunger and injustice. It called for new patterns of trade, aid and financial lending, in order to pull the world back from the very chaos which we now see emerging around us. Since that time, some individual countries have made good progress but the poorer countries of the world as a whole have moved far deeper into debt. Some Sahel region countries have moved into complete famine, while the world's wealthiest countries have become wealthier still, returning ever higher profits on their financial loans and dealings, and continuing to ignore all the warning signs of atmospheric and planetary disturbance which are resulting from our continued assault on the Earth's body, the 'Gaiasphere'.

If nothing has happened to turn the dream of a 'New International Economic Order' into a reality it is partly because the dream was something which had to be left up to government finance ministers to accomplish. It was a 'Think Global' idea without any equal and equivalent 'Act Local' activity. A 'new local economic order' could give the necessary grounding which the dreams so badly need.

Nothing of any deep human significance changes in our world without there being first a change in our own values. There are no technical, social or economic 'fixes' which can suddenly ensure us peace and plenty. As long as we are primarily interested in gathering and maintaining our own personal wealth to the neglect of anything else, we will continue to see children and their parents dying of hunger, young people wasting away their lives through enforced unemployment, and the steady genocide of the 'one-legged ones', the trees which live in our rainforests. A possible new local economic order will not be able to develop without a primary shift having first taken place in the values and the consciousness of the people involved.

My feelings tell me that this shift is happening. The huge reality of the famine in East Africa, people's new awareness about the very special value of the environment and their concern and compassion about unemployment, a desire by young people to do something that has inherent meaning and satisfaction, a sense of the madness of the expenditure on weaponry and the poverty and pain of so many millions sitting side by side, a growing acknowledgement that there are spiritual and loving realities in life as well as material and selfish ones—these and many other factors are all combining to shift people's subtle mindsets and to prepare the way for new ideas. Little may seem to be changing on the surface: the banks still extract their maximum profit from the poorest; the shops still sell hot-dogs grown on hamburger-farms carved out of the Amazon rainforest; the unemployment queues are still as long as ever—but underneath, things are changing. The Live-Aid concert in July 1985 allowed some of this change to show itself in public for the first time: people were intending not just to give food-aid, or to help dig a hundred thousand wells. They were intending those, plus something else: to feed the world. Positive intention of this magnitude is one indication of a large underground swell of changed attitudes and changed consciousness. It is still unformed, however. It does not yet (in 1985) properly understand how to translate intention into action. The desire is there for a completely different way of doing things, especially in the economic sphere, but the practical understanding of how it can be achieved is as yet lacking. This is the crucial importance of the set of ideas and initiatives which constitute the new local economic order.

The way we have done economics up to now has reflected the primacy of the task in which we have been engaged for the past few hundred years, during the period of the industrial age. We have been seeking material advance and development, discovery, exploration, reaching outwards all the time to learn what it is, this matter that we are made from, this planet that we live on, this universe that we exist within. We have been acting on masculine, 'yang' energy, seeking, thrusting, creating, destroying, imposing, separating, denying, attempting to put poverty and hardship and cruel fate behind us. We must never decry this task. We have overshot the mark, and now do not know why wealth and material well-being do not bring us constant happiness; and in our quest for material understanding and perfection we are now doing more damage than good; but these facts do not diminish the grandeur and quality of the goals we sought—and, in a major way, achieved.

This mentality built our economics in the same mould. We embraced concepts and assumptions which encouraged us to be aggressive, competitive, private and uncaring about the effect of our business operations upon nature. There is plenty enough planet to go around, we thought, so what does it matter if bits of it here and there get spoilt or exhausted? We need not care about such things as pollution—we can either bury our waste or simply pretend it isn't there, and nature will take care of the rest. As for our business operations—they were essentially private affairs, pursued for private gain and the glory of 'mankind'. The quest for profit and growth were natural goals to pursue. Free competition was the best method to allow for the maximum aggression and the fastest progress towards wealth. As for the workers, they were viewed as rather necessary evils, always in pursuit of more money and more perks and then holding the owners to ransom by forming unions and threatening strikes. You couldn't do business without them, and it was their wages which enabled them to buy the products which you needed to sell—but you did your best to hold them at bay and keep them happy by giving them occasional bonuses and holidays.

We all knew that business was a dirty affair. The kind, philanthropic businessmen were the exception, not the rule. The businessmen themselves knew it was an activity which forced them to act in hard, selfish and ignoble ways. Secretly, we hated ourselves for doing it all, and because of this, we kept it all the more private. Nobody expected to be helped—and, in addition, we learnt to resent interference of any kind. Rules, regulations and governments came to be hated objects. The free enterprise culture of 'John Wayne' cowboy economics did not like anyone telling it what it could or could not do. As for such things as the 'local economy'—well, it would simply look after itself. To think in terms of help or interference ran against the grain of the whole business culture, defensive and unable to give, hardened at the heart in self-protection against the sins that had to be committed in the name of profit and growth.

Thinking in anything except the short term made no sense either. The future could, after all, be expected to be much the same as the present—so why worry? And too much concern for things that were not materially real or achievable within a few years led to unhealthy speculations about things that had nothing to do with business. After all, the main purpose of life was material gain, wasn't it? So went the hidden business creed of the industrial age, keeping a tight upper lip against the unhappiness, cruelty, exploitation and wasted lives which everyone knew it entailed.

There were exceptions, of course, but it is these ideas, enshrined in Adam Smith's free market economic doctrines, which set the dominant tone of the way we lived and worked and did our business. In computerese, these assumptions were our 'embedded format commands'. In paradigm theory, they are the deep-level assumptions which underly the dominant paradigm of an age. They are thoughts that are not consciously thought out: we think them in our bellies. This gives them their strength—and also their obstinacy, long after they have ceased to be appropriate and long after the paradigm which they served has ceased to breath new life. It is these assumptions which are now being rejected by many people in the face of a completely new world situation. Industrial age, rest in peace.

*   *   *   *   *

During the long years of the industrial age, the main opposition to this set of values came through the socialist movements. These movements were characterised by a different vision, a soul-yearning for a peaceful, cooperative world—but also by a crucial need to defend workers' rights, by demands for more pay, by a generalised suspicion towards the whole class of owners, bankers and capitalists, by attacks on the essential nature of profit and profiteering (seen and emotionally felt as the extraction of surplus value), and by a broadly antipathetic attitude towards business as a whole. One polarity creates another. A right wing creates a left wing.

With some nervousness, I suggest that what is happening today is new. It transcends the divide between right and left. Both the emerging new values and the new local initiatives emerging on the ground are speaking a new language. It is a 'transpolitical' language. It draws on the best aspects of right-wing thought, involving belief in the value of initiative, enterprise and self-reliance, and the best aspects of left-wing thought, involving belief in the value of cooperation, sharing and caring for each other and for the environment. There are both left-wingers and right-wingers involved, as well as people with an environmental approach and people who have never thought things through very much. They are united by a joint sense of excitement at the challenge of doing something constructive at the local level. They are people who catch a whiff of something fresh and new, without even knowing too clearly what it is.

Let me give two examples to illustrate the way things are happening. Both are drawn from Canada.

The town of New Westminster is sited on the far west coast of Canada, close to Vancouver. Its biggest local industry is timber. In the recession of the late 1970s, demand fell severely and many workers were laid off. Two mills closed down. When demand picked up again, the mills brought in new technology in order to be competitive, instead of re-employing the workers. Unemployment stands at 20%, which represents 4,000 people. In November 1983, driven by concern about the future of New Westminster, 75 people representing every section of interest in the town were invited to a meeting by the principal of Douglas College, the local adult educational centre, and listened to a speaker from another community economic development initiative in Nanaimo, on Vancouver Island. Following this, 35 people became active in a local planning group, and in January 1984 they convened a public meeting at which they ensured that people representing local government, business, industry, labour, education, social services, unemployed people, professional groups and citizens associations were present.

A group was set up which subsequently became the Royal City Development Group, with a brief to achieve a sustained growth of employment opportunities through a community-supported economic development programme. They sought among other things to identify projects which would enhance the quality of life in the area, by cooperation between government, business, labour and voluntary and community groups. The college placed its resources at the group's disposal.

The group met monthly to discuss plans and possibilities, and to educate itself. At one meeting, they watched the BBC video on Mondragon, the very successful network of workers' cooperatives in northern Spain. The people present, including many from the business community, saw and were impressed by the evidence of how the Mondragon people had set up, among other things, their own cooperatives, product development centre and bank. They did not protest that no money was being returned to a separate group of shareholders, or that workers were telling their managers what they should do. They did not suspect some kind of a communist plot. They saw something successful, and started asking themselves if New Westminster could not do something similar for itself.

In the summer of 1984 they carried out a Community Economic Profile, providing a community inventory and a first planning step in what would hopefully become a long-term economic development strategy. By mid-1985, plans were under way for the establishment of a Centre for Enterprise Development, based at the college, which would offer a business information and referral service, a business educational resource, a counselling service, a physical development space or test bed for inventors and entrepreneurs to try out ideas, a business office-systems support centre, a 'mentoring' service to provide one-to-one support for new entrepreneurs, and a 'New Enterprise Club'. They have also helped set up a job-club at the unemployment action centre, and have drawn up plans for the development of new cooperative housing to meet the needs of single parents and disabled groups, on a mixed income basis. All this in their first 18 months of existence.

On the far opposite coast of Canada, at the northern end of Nova Scotia, lies the island of Cape Breton, originally settled by people from the western islands of Scotland at the time of the clearances and the potato famine. The Scottish musical tradition is in excellent shape, but not so the local economy, which has been depressed for years, ever since the coalmines on which the wealth of the area was based began to close down. The coalmine owners used to own everything, even the company store, and left behind them among local people a very negative attitude towards business, which was associated with exploitation, and simultaneously a dependency upon outside employers. The official unemployment figure for the island is 29.5%, which may hide a true figure closer to 45%. The Canadian government has now decided that it will make Cape Breton a special test-bed for new approaches to economic development. Their first move has been to offer special tax-breaks to outside firms as an incentive for them to move onto the island. This same policy was tried in 1971, when eight firms moved in. Not one is still there, some having moved to places where they could pay lower wages and not have to deal with trade unions. Among the companies which may possibly move to Cape Breton is Littons, a Canadian corporation which does a lot of military work, including manufacturing parts for cruise missiles. This, then, is the challenge to the Cape Bretoners: find a way of creating your own economic development on the island, or accept companies like Littons and wave goodbye to your consciences.

Cape Breton's past shows up all the shadows of traditional 'cowboy' economics—exploitation, dependency, bad will, confrontation, rip-offs. The Canadian government, in seeking to bring development to the area, draws on the old mind-set. If firms won't move in freely, then pay them to move in. 'More of the same' is their answer. Like other governments, they also like the 'megaproject' approach to problems. A heavy water plant was built on Cape Breton to provide jobs and to play a part in Canada's struggling nuclear industry. In its whole life, not one pint of heavy water was ever sold, and each job that was created cost $171,000 (£100,000). This contrasts with a figure of only £2,000 per job created through the 'new economic' community-based approaches in the UK, such as enterprise agencies and cooperative development agencies. The heavy water plant has now closed down.

'Vision' is a community group based in Sydney, Cape Breton, which is seeking a very different type of development. Their goal is a development which springs from local people's own perceptions of their needs, and from their own imagination and skill. The words and phrases they use are 'regional cooperation', 'innovation', 'participation' and 'community-based economic development'.

In order to understand Cape Breton, you have to know not only that it is an isle of exceptional beauty, full of mountain, sea, sky and music, but also that the eight autonomous municipalities have a 200-year-old tradition of being jealous and suspicious of each other, which stems from the times when the coalmine owners used deliberately to set the different communities off against each other to stimulate production. 'Vision' has worked firstly to bring everyone together for the greater gain of the whole area, and to overcome the divisiveness. To this end, they selected 50 key people from the Cape Breton community (labour unions, the university, the eight municipal leaders, womens' groups, youth groups, business leaders, etc) and brought them together for a three-day 'Search conference' in which they all explored the question 'What kind of community do we want 20 years from now?' They worked in five groups of ten, and drew up lists of what they felt were the ten best things and the ten worst things about Cape Breton, with the instruction that each group had to reach towards consensus. When their results were revealed, every group had chosen identically: they all stated their full belief in the human and natural resources of Cape Breton, and they all hated the bickering and fragmentation. They later drew up a list of 100 different initiatives which they could take for the overall good of the community, and then formed a steering group asking it to put together a plan. All 50 people are still involved, which shows the real strength of this kind of deep-level participation exercise.

We are familiar with the experience of three-day workshops in which people share and explore their own lives and in which they become very close because they begin to meet at the level of the heart. The same thing can happen when people come together to share their worries and hopes for their own local economy. This is one way in which new local economic orders will be born.

'Vision' has to move fast, because it faces a real pressure of time if it is to keep up people's hopes; and it needs to move slowly in order to keep everyone involved. It is always so easy for a small group of people to take a plan and rush off ahead with it, leaving everyone else behind. 'Vision' has formed task groups on small business, municipal cooperation, communications, labour, industry, training and technology, youth, tourism and culture, and they are looking among other things at the development of an enterprise centre. They are financing their work through a central government grant, which pays for a small staff. They are consciously aware that their approach has to be 'transpolitical', involving everyone for the greater good of the whole community, drawing on beliefs both in enterprise and initiative, and in cooperation.

*   *   *   *   *

It is in observing developments such as those above—and they can be repeated many times, in communities all over the world—that I find confirmation for my belief that something is astir. Here are people thinking, talking, planning and doing economics, local economics, but doing it from such a different basis. The old attitudes are gone. There is no more talk of private gain, private profit, owners and workers, suspicion and fear. Here the words and phrases are 'we', 'our own initiative', and 'our own vision'. The values have undergone a complete sea-change.

The people at 'Vision' knew that their desire was for the people of Cape Breton to build up their own local economy, coloured in their own colours, but they had also to work out what they felt about the 60 new outside businesses which the Ottawa government said were willing to come to the island. The first reaction was suspicion—a feeling of despair, of 'not again', knowing that the last time outside businesses moved in they soon moved out again, leaving behind them anger and bad will. What now?

In discussion, the 'Vision' people realised that what they needed to do was draw up a code of business ethics. If the new businesses were willing to adhere to this, it would allow them to feel welcome. After all, if a transplant takes successfully, it becomes a local business. For a transplant to be successful, however, the heart has to be transplanted too—and, in business terms, the heart means the ownership. What was discussed, while I was there, was the possibility of the firms being invited in on the following conditions: that they adhered to a code of ecological behaviour; that they took measures to involve the workers whom they employed at every level, from participation on the shop-floor to participation on the managing board to participation as worker shareholders; that they agreed to adopt a proactive policy to ensure that ownership steadily moved into the hands of local, Cape Breton people; that they undertook no work which was socially, ecologically or planetarily harmful. These were only private discussions—nothing was on the table at this stage, and the group knew full well that they had to choose their words very carefully in order not to lose people along the way. The point is made, however: when a community starts thinking for itself economically, it comes up with a very different overall agenda than when a private board of shareholders thinks for itself.

The expectation of a new code of ethics and behaviour applies not only to business transplants, but also to the new wave of businesses which can be set up with help from the emerging local community-based business support systems. In the past, the community was never expected to help local businesses: they were out for their own private gain, so why should anyone think of wanting to help them? But now it is seen as being necessary to help people to launch new businesses for the sake of the whole local economy. In return for their support, the community can reasonably ask for something back: that the businesses adhere to a new code of business ethics which embraces ecological responsibility, community involvement, participation and hopefully co-ownership by workers, and responsibility towards the rest of the planet, especially the South. The Greater London Enterprise Board expects this kind of reciprocal deal: businesses which seek its help cannot receive assistance unless they agree to take part in 'Enterprise Planning', a joint process which involves both workers and managers. They have encountered very little resistance to this expectation.

As we move towards a conclusion, it is possible to pick out five particular themes which must be essential components of this emerging new local economic order.

The first of these is that the new economic pattern must be rooted in love for the place. When the place itself is loved, it becomes natural to want to build up a local economic order which expresses that love, which amplifies and increases the character, quality and beauty of the place and its people. The economy needs then to reflect the special quality of the place itself, including its history, its present and its potential future.

The second theme is that business can become a path of service, rather than of greed and selfishness. We can and must reclaim business as a possible spiritual path through which visions can be realised and dreams unfolded, both in terms of the product or service offered and in terms of the way in which everyone involved in the business can be expected to grow and become inwardly wealthy and fulfilled as people. This is happening already within many of the new cooperatives. It can—and will—happen within all kinds of business, once our values begin to change in a wholesale way, as we properly leave behind the industrial age with its own needs and values.

The third theme is that a community can and should give support to its businesses, in a variety of ways. Britain is full of new community-based initiatives which are developing ways to help local businesses and to assist new businesses to form. When these are placed together into a coordinated pattern, we begin to see a new kind of order appearing at a higher level, replacing the existing order of business and economic behaviour which is currently crumbling and under great stress. The failure rate among cooperatives, for instance, has been estimated at only 5% a year, which is considerably better than figures quoted by the UK Department of Industry for all businesses. The Briarpatch Network in San Francisco, which is a wide mutual support network for its members, also reports a failure rate far lower than the norm. The new values produce better material and financial results, as well as happier people.

The fourth theme is that we can expect our new businesses—and, hopefully, over a period of time, existing businesses—to adhere to new values as expressed in new codes of business ethics concerning the local environment, the local community, the people working directly in the business, patterns of ownership and control, and the relationship of the business with the planet as a whole. As and when a community develops its own sources of loan finance, as London has done through the

Greater London Enterprise Board, adherence to these codes can then be expected in tangible terms, as a condition of receiving financial support.

The fifth theme is that these new local economies need to embrace long-term thinking and planning in the fields of housing, food production, energy, the environment, trees, human needs and the host of other areas which are of concern to us all. Short-term thinking is a natural expression of selfishness; long-term thinking is a natural expression of love, whether it is for one's family, one's local place, community and economy, or the planet as a whole.

*   *   *   *   *

The new values, which speak among other things of care for the Earth, long-term sustainability, and cooperation as well as competition, are growing in strength all the time. New practical local economic initiatives are constantly being developed. There is at present no conscious awareness of deliberate overlap, and no language with which the overlap, as it develops, can be clearly expressed. The term 'transpolitical' is completely new.

The movement of both values and initiatives is clearly to be seen, however, and in places such as New Westminster and Cape Breton the overlap can be seen emerging in practice. My own interest is in the relevance of new local economic thinking not just for the countries of the North but also for the countries of the South, which desperately need a new development philosophy and practice, and also for China and the countries of Eastern Europe, which are searching for ways in which they can release new energy within their economies without adopting the whole capitalist path. The path of development outlined above does offer a region or country a way forward which allows for the virtues of enterprise and initiative and the virtues of cooperation and caring to exist side-by-side, as it is only natural that they should. The new local economic order approach can offer us a solution to our ecological disorders, to our problems of unemployment, to the desperate imbalance of North and South, to the ideological warfare between East and West and to the deep inner need that we have to be able to live and work in a spiritually meaningful and rewarding way. If this seems to be claiming a lot, it is only making a claim in proportion to the scale of change possible once we shift our values away from the old, distrustful, aggressive style into a new, trustful, caring, supportive one.

Some people will say this is impossible. Some will say it is impossible to feed the world. We do not need to hear those doubts. We have only one choice that we can possibly make: to believe in the full extent of our own as-yet-unrealised human possibility. To do anything less is to settle for second best. In fact, it is far worse—it is to settle for the continued pain, chaos and likely destruction of the Earth. We have to reach for the highest dreams of all: then we will attain them. *THAT \THE IDEA - ON WHICH AMERICAN WAS ESTABLISHED)*

(1)*Details of some of the best initiatives in the UK can be found in* The LEDIS Sheets *which come from the Local Economic Development Information Service, The Planning Exchange, 186 Bath St, Glasgow G2 4HG. (Price £25 pa).*

Community Enterprise in the Highlands and Islands

Roy Pedersen

Roy Pedersen is Social Development Officer in the Policy and Research Division of the Highlands and Islands Development Board based in Inverness, Scotland. A major aspect of his work is encouraging local communities to develop their own solutions to the problems of social and economic decline.

A few years ago the Highlands and Islands Development Board, the organisation for which I work, undertook a scheme for encouraging community enterprise in the Highlands and Islands of Scotland. I would like briefly to describe the Highlands and Islands and then go on to explain a little bit about the scheme and give an example of one of the cooperatives which have been set up under it. There is no typical example for setting up a community business—each one is a law unto itself—but this one will give as good an idea as any of the process.

The Highlands and Islands is a vast region of mountains, lochs, glens and about one hundred inhabited islands at the very edge of Europe, covering just under half the land area of Scotland and approximately one sixth of the United Kingdom. Although it is an area larger than the Netherlands or Belgium, it has a population of only 350,000 people and an average population of 24.3 persons per square mile, compared with 168 for Scotland as a whole and 610 for Great Britain. The largest town is Inverness with a population of 40,000; no other settlement is larger than 12,000 and there are not even many of that size.

This part of Scotland has a long history of decline. It is an extremely beautiful area but the human story is a very tragic one. In 1857 the population was 423,000; by 1966 because of continuous economic decline and out-migration it had sunk to under 300,000. The special circumstances of the Highlands and Islands have been recognised in a series of special measures and legislation dating from the 19th century.

91

As part of this process the Highlands and Islands Development Board was set up by Act of Parliament in 1965, its principal objectives being to assist the people of the Highlands and Islands to improve their economic and social conditions and to enable the area to play a more effective part in the economic and social development of the nation.

The Board, which comprises four executive and three non-executive members appointed by the Secretary of State for Scotland, is based in Inverness and has a staff of about 240 people. In the main island groups and the more distant parts of the mainland we now have six or seven area officers who act as the door through which local people can make contact with the Board. The annual budget we get from Treasury is between £30 million and £40 million. In some ways that is a lot of money but in comparison to other government agencies it is in fact very little, and possibly because of this the Board gets away with being more flexible than is normal for a government agency.

In pursuing its work the Board operates in three main fields. It provides financial assistance to businesses expanding or setting up in the area; it undertakes development projects such as the provision of advance factories, sometimes in very remote areas; and it acts both in an advisory capacity and in the area of social research and planning. The power to give financial assistance is entirely at the Board's discretion, within certain guidelines laid down by central government. The Board can decide whether or not to assist a person or company or group and, if so, to what extent.

The community cooperative scheme is part of the work of the HIDB, but I would like to stress that it involves only about 2% of the Board's budget and personnel, so it is a relatively small part of the whole operation. The international officially recognised definition of a cooperative is a group of people who organise to provide themselves with some service or goods in accordance with six cooperative principles laid down in the 1840s. First of all, membership of a cooperative is open and voluntary and there should be no discrimination on grounds of factors like religion, sex or politics. Secondly, control of the organisation is democratic on the basis of one-person-one-vote, rather than proportional to the amount of money invested. Thirdly, in order to prevent speculation in cooperative shares, payment of interest on share capital is limited. Unlike putting your money into nickel mines in Australia, where you can really make a fortune, you'll never make a lot of money out of investing in co-ops; rather people will invest in a co-op because they want to partake of the goods and services it provides. The fourth principle is that profits of the organisation are distributed in accordance with trade done; fifthly, cooperatives have an educative purpose; and finally, there should be cooperation among cooperatives. These principles are recognised internationally and on the planet as a whole there are some 350 million people involved in cooperatives—that's about one in twelve of the Earth's population—so it's big stuff.

The community cooperative scheme in the Highlands and Islands originated after the HIDB had been in operation for ten years or so. During that first ten years the population decline was arrested and reversed; since 1966 it has risen from 300,000 to 350,000 largely due to net in-migration of population. However, while this upsurge was affecting certain areas, in the more remote parts on the edge of the Highlands and Islands the population was still declining. Young people were leaving and marrying in other areas; few children were being born into some of those small communities with the result that such communities were dying. All this was happening despite the Board's most generous packages of assistance being made available. People were not coming forward with development ideas. Moreover, the relatively small number of incoming businesses the Board managed to attract to places like the Western Isles in the late 60s and early 70s failed—by and large because of their remoteness from decision-making; often the company head office would be in the south or midlands of England. This happened, for example, in the case of a company manufacturing spectacle frames on the island of Barra; the lines of communication between management and workforce were simply too extended, and there were also cultural differences which the telephone can't easily resolve.

The Western Isles is an egalitarian community, and entrepreneurship has been slow to develop. The language is Gaelic, human activity is removed from the mainstream of business development and crofting is a way of life. Basically, a croft is a smallholding on which it is not generally possible to earn the whole of one's living, so the crofter turns his or her hand to other occupations also, whether those be fishing, being the local postman or whatever. The crofting township is a very special social unit with a strong tradition of doing things communally. The crofters rent land in common on which they keep their sheep and cattle and they control that land through a Grazings Committee; moreover, cutting peats for fuel, harvest work and sheep dipping and clipping are all done communally. There is also a tradition of people not wanting to stand out above their neighbours for fear of ridicule. So if someone has a good idea with regard to development, there's a tendency not to want to make it known in case their neighbours criticise them.

In pondering this general problem of lack of development in areas which needed it most, the idea of cooperatives emerged. If people are used to working communally and if they are reluctant to come up with development ideas as individuals, why not see if they can be encouraged to come forward with such ideas collectively? And so the community cooperative scheme was born

A community cooperative is a business—usually multi-functional—run in accordance with cooperative principles for local benefit and directly owned and controlled by the community in which it operates. Its activities may be social in character but it must make a profit overall. Membership is open to all adult residents (and former residents) of the community served, and representatives of a substantial proportion of households would normally subscribe to shares in the cooperative. As well as receiving any dividend or other benefit which membership of the co-op may confer, shareholders are entitled to elect a management committee and agree broadly the direction to be pursued. Because of the one-person-one-vote principle local democratic control takes precedence over powerful financial interests.

The co-op's management committee sets policies, targets and budgets and looks after the general development of the business, reporting regularly to the members. To handle day-to-day management of the cooperative, the committee normally appoints a paid professional manager who in turn is responsible for engaging any employees necessary to enable the co-op to carry out its work.

There is almost no limit to the range of trading activities a community cooperative can carry out as long as, when taken together, they have the support of the community and are likely to earn sufficient income to cover operating costs, including the wages and expenses of the manager and other staff. During the first few years at least, any surplus would usually be invested in the co-op rather than being distributed to members in the form of interest or bonus.

The Highlands and Islands Development Board assists new community cooperatives both as a general support structure and in various specific ways. One is an establishment grant—typically about £20,000—which is a pound-for-pound matching of the amount raised by the cooperative in local share capital. The Board will also pay a manager's salary for a period of years until the business gets going.

Once established, the cooperative can approach the Board with any project under the normal grants and loans scheme available for developers. Financial assistance for such projects can be as high as 50%—or even 70% under exceptional conditions. Funds are also available for the training of cooperative managers, employees and committee members.

Bureaucracies like to surround themselves with concrete and glass and make themselves comfortable—and the HIDB is no exception; but this makes it all the more difficult to undertake development in the kinds of areas we deal with. How do people from those areas find someone in a concrete fortress who is likely to be sympathetic to their ideas? And likewise how does a person working in the fortress find somebody out there who has good ideas?

One such person was a crofter's wife from a particular island community who left school when she was 14, brought up her family and works the croft. I got a message from her one day that her community was interested in building a hall and could the Board help. They wanted more than just an ordinary hall; they wanted a centre for the community where various activities could take place and where people could meet and undertake business. The Board does help as a matter of course with village halls, but if the community wanted to attach a business structure to it as well, it seemed there might be a possibility for a community cooperative.

The story of the idea for a village hall in this community had been a long one. In 1901 the local teacher died and left £200 for the building of such a hall but the idea was rejected by the local churches, who were convinced it would encourage sinful activity. Every couple of decades somebody would promote the idea of building a hall, and then the idea would be crushed by the church. The same thing happened in 1978. A public meeting was called at which 100 people attended out of a community of 600 and it was decided a hall would be a good thing. The following Sunday, however, one of the local ministers preached against it. Suddenly people started backing off the idea. But for the first time in 70 years an individual—the crofter's wife—had the courage to say, "Well, if you're against us, you're against us, but I think we should go ahead anyway." Despite further adverse pressure for a time, opposition finally crumbled and the project went ahead. It takes great personal courage to stand against such opinion in a small community.

Gradually a network of people built up and one of the key figures in the whole process was the architect. He was young, his parents were from the community and he was willing to undertake the work—not only of designing the hall but also of acting as clerk of works.

My job to a large extent concerns finding ways of getting different portions of money together in order to fund projects. One of the problems in this case was that in order to get the special grants obtainable from the Scottish Office and local authority for the setting up of village halls, those involved had to form some sort of charitable association; on the other hand, to obtain the HIDB grant for community cooperatives, they had to be a commercial organisation. The two are incompatible legally. However, the community also had a sympathetic lawyer and he and I between us eventually devised a structure which consisted of two legal entities—the hall trust and the community cooperative. The hall trust actually owns the building but the community cooperative has prepaid about thirty years of rent for use of it.

The community reckoned they could raise £20,000 from their own resources. In fact, they raised £26,000, which is a considerable achievement. Virtually every family subscribed £25 by way of share capital to the cooperative and besides that they held sponsored events to raise money. There was a lot of work to be done in applying to the Board for funds. The local committee had to produce things like cash flows, projected accounts, a business plan and so on, which was not so easy for a rural community of this kind, but the great thing about this cooperative and others is to observe the personal development of the people taking part in it, the growth in skills and self-confidence. Anyway, the business plan was eventually approved and the cooperative was registered.

The hall, now fully operational, really is a community centre. The main part of it is the size of two badminton courts. Sports, dances and a youth club are held there. There is also a Gaelic playgroup for children, which is very important in a place where the main language is under intense erosive pressure from television and other media; in other playgroups in the West Highlands where English has been used the result has been a rapid deterioration of Gaelic in the children. The building also houses the community's grocery shop and a restaurant which seats 40 people. The restaurant is a wonderful place for people to meet and is also a means of making money from tourists in the summer, which is a source of income to keep the cooperative going and to create capital for future projects.

In the Highlands and Islands as a whole there are now some 20 community cooperatives, of which the majority are multi-functional with full-time paid managers. The total turnover is in excess of £2 million. A wide variety and mix of business is undertaken but retailing in one form or another accounts for some 85% of all activity. A number of co-ops are turning to productive activities such as salmon farming, mechanised peat extraction and light manufacturing, while a range of services such as transport, catering and community hall management are socially important in a number of cases but represent a small proportion of revenue. Some cooperatives are involved in small-scale marketing—mainly knitwear, crafts and tourism. One co-op is now vigorously pursuing fish marketing, and this may develop into a substantial business.

Community cooperative development methods have changed in the light of experience. Initially the stimulus to set up a cooperative was typically a feeling locally that 'something' needed to be done to reverse the declining fortunes of a community. It has sometimes been difficult for cooperatives originating this way to find a mix of activities sufficiently profitable to cover management overheads by the time the HIDB management grant ceases. Unfortunate choices of 'core' projects can exacerbate the problem—for example, retailing agricultural requisites yields notoriously low margins. In more recent years community cooperatives have tended to emerge out of some specific local development opportunity, such as the threatened closure of the community's shop. This approach seems to foster tighter management and more rapid progress to viability.

The Board has always encouraged cooperation among cooperatives where practicable and there have been a number of assemblies of community cooperatives and joint seminars to discuss issues of mutual interest. The creation of a federation has been mooted for some years but the idea, while desirable in principle, is still considered premature by the cooperatives themselves.

Since the start of the scheme the HIDB has emphasised the need for cooperatives to be profitable if long term survival is to be assured, and great stress has been placed on sound financial management. It has proved extraordinarily difficult to establish effective financial control systems in isolated communities where readily available professional and business expertise and advice is invariably absent. A number of training initiatives have been tried over the years but their success has been limited. The HIDB is now using specialised and area staff backed up by consultant accountants to install and monitor management systems, and this approach is beginning to show results.

Broadly speaking, about one-third of the existing co-ops are now in the black, another third are making progress towards break-even, and the remaining third are either experiencing difficulty in finding a route to viability or are at such an early stage that it is not possible to make a judgment. To date, no community cooperative assisted under the scheme has failed, although two small single-function co-ops became moribund and were wound up, having been unable to find a viable *raison d'être* or to attract sufficient community support.

In the early days of the scheme the HIDB took a strict line regarding conformity to the laid-down multi-functional model, but now a rather more flexible approach prevails and the setting up process and assistance available are to a greater extent adjusted to suit local needs and timescales. It is likely that new variants to the model will continue to emerge, stimulated in part by the experience of community businesses in other parts of Scotland. Already a couple of embryonic multi-purpose community enterprises exist in the Highlands and Islands which are not registered under the community cooperative model rules but which share the key features of voluntary membership open to the community and democratic control. A number of legal structures are available for community enterprises, of which the company limited by guarantee is probably the most popular alternative to the community cooperative. One distinction is that companies limited by guarantee may not distribute profits to members.

Whatever the legal structure, the development value of a multi-purpose community enterprise lies in its ability, once operational, to take advantage of new development opportunities as they emerge. This is beginning to happen in a number of areas, and in some cases separate companies wholly or partly owned by the community enterprise have been established to undertake specific new trading activities. This type of arrangement has the advantage of to some extent protecting the community enterprise from the effects of failure of a large, risky, new venture. It also affords the opportunity for joint ventures with, for example, local entrepreneurs should the community enterprise have insufficient capital.

In the six years since the first Highlands and Islands community cooperative started trading, the struggle for commercial viability has been, of necessity, paramount. Such achievements as there have been to date are testimony to the commitment, skill and determination of what now amounts to hundreds of individuals, paid and unpaid, in some of the most far flung parts of a peripheral region.

There is no doubt, however, that the quest for viability has tended to overshadow the need to cultivate the involvement of the ordinary community members. In the long run this involvement is vital if community cooperatives or other forms of community enterprise are to be genuinely 'of' the community. With this in mind the HIDB are currently considering what steps can be taken to improve links between management and membership. Total community cooperative membership has grown to well over 3,000, representing local capital subscription totalling over a quarter of a million pounds, which is a power base worth harnessing. Without the level of financial assistance and extended support available from the HIDB, few if any of the earlier community cooperatives would have emerged—but equally without community commitment no progress could ever have been made.

Nowadays, because of staffing constraints, the HIDB approach to community enterprise tends to await approaches from community groups with development proposals rather than actively seeking them out. Nevertheless, four steering committees are currently assessing the potential for new community enterprises in their areas. The idea of community self help may be starting to take root as a credible method of undertaking socially relevant economic development.

Easterhouse:
Acting for Ourselves

Chris Elphick

Chris Elphick is Organising Secretary of the Easterhouse Festival Society, a community-based project in Glasgow which for the past several years has contributed to the revitalisation of a depressed urban area by fostering community spirit and encouraging creativity through arts, crafts, sports, social events and small business activities.

The Easterhouse Festival Society has a motto: "Let us act for ourselves." Maybe we should change that to "We *are* acting for ourselves," because that is what is happening at Easterhouse in Glasgow. It is interesting at this conference to hear people coming up with all different kinds of theories, but in Easterhouse we are not talking about theory. It is a place where theory is going to come out of practice.

Easterhouse is a large, 25-year-old housing scheme on the northeast edge of Glasgow. It was built so that people could be moved from the tenements where housing conditions no longer seemed suitable for people to live in. Fifty thousand of us live there on the edge of the city, and there are five of these estates around Glasgow, with a total population of 300,000.

Forty per cent of the male working-age population of Easterhouse is unemployed. There are whole streets where nobody gets up in the morning to go to work of any type, whether paid or not. You can imagine the effect that has on people. It actually destroys them. But now people are saying, "That's enough. It's not going to happen any more. We are going to turn the process around."

Easterhouse is a community that lacks facilities. For those 50,000 people we have five pubs. A small village often has more than that. We have *one* cafe. There are no cultural facilities at all, and no industrial base. The housing is uniformly drab; the environment is not exciting.

You walk along the streets; they're dull. The shops are dull too, and there are a lot of boarded-up houses. Many of these empty buildings have been up for not much more than ten years. They're going to be pulled down, but the local authority can't afford to do it, so people are paid to look after them. Of course, these people, walking around in uniforms in an area where people are sitting about with nothing to do, become targets.

Another problem is that everything is centralised. The philosophy behind Easterhouse was that they were going to create a town in the countryside. But can you imagine a town with 50,000 people and nothing else? In a real town, people interact; they move around it; they go to different parts to do different things. That doesn't happen in Easterhouse. You go to the centre to buy your food, or to go to the swimming pool (which we finally got after ten years of trying) or to the police station.

There's nothing to do in Easterhouse. Who can blame people if they turn to glue-sniffing or heroin? There are 12-year-old kids addicted to heroin. Can you imagine giving heroin to your 12-year-old son or daughter? It's being given away in the schools by the kind pushers, so that the children will get addicted to it and then go out and steal money to put into the pockets of the dealers—who never use heroin themselves of course.

The kids of Easterhouse are not being educated for life at all; they're not getting an education which enables them to believe that they have strength and individuality and that they can grow. That has to change, and the people of Easterhouse are beginning to change it themselves.

Poverty is not a fashionable word these days, particularly in government circles. The sort of poverty we are talking about in Easterhouse is a poverty of expectation. Very sadly, people have come to expect less and less of themselves, of their friends, of their families and of the people who provide resources and facilities. For example, for a small group in Easterhouse to get a hut for their community to meet in, it may take three years of hard work and knocking on people's doors, and they end up with a cheap, substandard building that nobody else wanted. They're delighted; they say, "That's great. Thanks very much." But it's an absolute disgrace, and it only happens because these are large areas where people have no power whatsoever.

Something we should all remember is that the real changes we're going to see in our society will happen when the people who at the moment don't have power—or believe they don't—suddenly realise that they do. When these people rediscover some self-respect, confidence, access to knowledge, then there are going to be changes which cannot be predicted. A lot of people are not going to like what happens, because those changes are not written about in textbooks—and quite rightly, because the people involved in those changes are never going to write textbooks.

I'm talking about a situation that's far from comfortable, where people really do have to struggle all the time because they are determined they are going to improve things. They are determined to have control over their own lives and destinies, and that they're no longer going to be manipulated. Now maybe that ideal is a long way off, but it's what we're moving towards. In Easterhouse people know that nobody has done them any good in the past 25 years, no matter what the political party.

For a community to do anything, they have to feel a solidarity with what has gone before. In Glasgow particularly there have been many demonstrations and marches demanding work; and people in Easterhouse do feel part of the working class history of the city. For example, several people from Easterhouse, including a rock band, joined the 'People's March for Jobs' from Glasgow to London, in support for what they see at the moment as the struggle for jobs. They have ideas about a better future, but we must protect the present as well, and it's important that people feel they can join together in solidarity to protect what's here at the moment.

Although Easterhouse is a very poor area, we managed to raise between £7,000 and £8,000 over a period of seven months for striking miners and their families. People gave money they really needed for themselves, but they did it because there is such a strong feeling of togetherness. One of the positive things happening is that people are using that unity to move from reaction—fighting *against* things—to positive action. They're saying, "We are now going to create something for ourselves, something we can fight *for*, something that gives us hope for the future."

There is an important link between the regeneration of communities by the people themselves and creativity and the arts—not arts in an elitist sense but in the widest possible creative sense. It's easy to look at Easterhouse and think, "Good God, what a place!" But within that place something very remarkable and important for the future is happening. Not everybody is succumbing to poverty and despair. There are poets in that area, there are painters and musicians; there was a chap doing wrought-iron work in his bedroom until his house caught fire and the fire brigade put a stop to it. There's an energy moving. It's a lot easier, I'm sure, for people to have a vision and feel the energy to do something about it in a peaceful and problem-free place, but it's truly remarkable that that energy exists in an area like Easterhouse where you would think the people could just die off and nobody would know about it.

The Easterhouse Festival Society was formed in 1978. The word 'festival' is the most crucial word. Part of the society's aim, as written down seven years ago, is "to celebrate life in our community, to raise questions about the community and to take action to bring sections of the community together." We are there to offer encouragement to people to confront their problems and to engage themselves in more fruitful searches for solutions. Our work stresses creativity and imagination and is concerned with providing opportunities for people to explore their creative talents and potential, to unlock their innermost hopes and aspirations and to help them open doors which replace despair and dereliction with hope and dignity.

No-one has all the answers to the problems of areas like Easterhouse, but the Festival Society is a contribution of the right sort because it encourages and supports people's desire to do things for themselves, and unless that desire can be tapped and encouraged, there can be no solutions. The answer in the end must come from within, from inside these areas.

Easterhouse has always had a bad name, and part of our job at every possible moment is to make sure that people know about the good things going on there. I'd like to give a challenge to the media: to tell people truly and honestly about what is going on in the Easterhouses of the world. I read an article in a Scottish newspaper recently about a group of English civil servants who were going to be moved to Glasgow. They were taken in a big posh coach around the west of Scotland to see where they would like to live. The article says: "They shuddered as they passed through Easterhouse. 'One of our schemes which you won't want to live in,' said a Glasgow planning department official. He said that Easterhouse was part of the things that were wrong with Glasgow." That's brilliant, isn't it? These people hadn't even been to the place and they were being turned off it. He didn't tell them about the mosaic we've created, or about our employment work or education work. Oh no. He told them it was a place they didn't want to go to. And that is the message that everybody in the media seems to want to get across. They've got to stop destroying us. They're not going to win, by the way. In fact, they could actually help us if they wished.

The creative work we're doing includes running a rock concert with local bands every year. The area is full of talented people who, very sadly because of the way our society is at the moment, are not going to have the opportunity to develop those talents, unless we create those opportunities ourselves—and that is what we are doing. Many young people in the area have had the opportunity through our work and the work of others to do this.

A great deal of individual creative work goes on too, such as photography, the visual arts, video etc. Two unemployed girls in the Festival Society have built a puppet booth and are starting to do puppet shows, creating work for themselves out of their interest. And of course they're carrying a message for Easterhouse, that this has come out of Easterhouse; this is *us* doing this. People also get together regularly to read poetry they've written. One of our local poets, Freddy, who writes about the working class history of Glasgow, has had books published.

A lot of our work is with kids. They are the future. They are great fun to work with and they really enjoy getting involved in Festival activities and celebrations. We also work with old people. The elderly are a very underrated but important part of the community. They have so much experience and wisdom to offer the younger people, but very few people are attempting to work out how they can be productive.

Much of our work takes place in the pubs. The pubs are important places where people go and meet. The local authorities build community centres and suchlike, but people don't naturally go to them—they go to the pubs, the shops and the betting shop. That's where people meet and where ideas are talked about.

We also do a lot with sports. There are many talented footballers, boxers and darts players in the area, and again people are having the opportunity to develop their talents and skills.

We are involved in all kinds of work, but the creative work, the performing work—the circus work, if you like—is always part of what we do. There isn't much to celebrate in Easterhouse, but what there is to celebrate is the people and their strength. That's why people come out on the street and why we bring in theatre and drama and so on. It's all linked with a process of change.

We do some crazy things as well. For example, we created a swimming pool overnight in the car park of the local shopping centre and turned the area into a seaside for the day. We even made sticks of Easterhouse rock. We like organising large outdoor events that bring people together. The one thing that people in Easterhouse don't want to be reminded of is the poverty. They live in it every day, morning, noon and night. These events are an opportunity for people to come together in a situation where there are no pressures, and no-one is standing up and saying, "This is what to do," or "You've got to follow this or vote for that." None of that. They're enjoying themselves. We're being creative together, and that leads on to all sorts of things.

One of the most important ways of putting across to people our feelings of anger and frustration is through drama—not through Shakespeare or plays that other people have written, but through plays that have been written in Easterhouse about what it's like to live there. Every year we tour the plays around our own area and Glasgow and to the Edinburgh Fringe Festival and so on.

We sometimes do Shakespeare. We went to the island of Iona for a week once and put on a production of *Macbeth* starting from nothing on the first day and ending with the production on the last day, involving everybody on the island at the time. We used energy, creativity, imagination, guts, all sorts of things, plus a lot of bullying and so on. If you're doing something on an island like Iona, you can't go and get resources. You've got to use what's there. There's a message in that for work in any other community.

At this point there are 40 to 50 people working full time with the Festival Society in all sorts of different areas of development. A handful of those are paid—not necessarily a good situation but that's how it is. Every now and again it's important to say 'thank you' to everybody, and we bring together all those who work with us and take them out for the day—and of course we have a good old drink.

Because we're fighting extremes in terms of poverty and so on, it has to be fun. There has to be a vision of excitement, because that's what's going to carry us forward. And of course our work with kids does as well. Our investment in the future is kids growing up in an imaginative and creative manner.

Another thing we are planning is to convert an empty factory into an arts-cum-sports-cum-business centre. It will create in the region of 150 jobs and provide a facility that doesn't exist in the east end of Glasgow. Interestingly, the local authority had a plan for this ten years ago, but it's been on the shelf ever since. We decided a year ago to convert the place and we plan to start work on it at the end of this year. All we need to do it is £1,000,000. We're working on that at the moment, and it will come. The important thing about this centre is that we're going to combine the arts, sports and business. Most people in Easterhouse are not used to doing anything other than working for somebody else, but that thinking is changing. It's not going to change through theory or rhetoric, though; it's going to be changed through the doing.

We have also started exploring new relationships. We're working with the business sector and have created the Easterhouse Partnership between the business sector and the community. A lot of ideas are coming from the community and we're asking the business sector to find out how they can be paid for. All we're asking for, in fairness, is for businesses to put something back into the area, because they take a lot out. The betting shop—Ladbroke's—for example, is the busiest in western Europe, although Easterhouse is one of the poorest areas. We want to say to Ladbroke's, "Come on, you have a social responsibility here."

The dull, drab environment of Easterhouse needs to be brightened up—and by people who live locally. We decided that one of our projects would be to transform a certain wall and the area round about it, including a pub called the Casbah. Scottish and Newcastle Breweries came into the partnership and did up the pub for about £50,000. In fact, it's our relationship with them that got the Easterhouse Partnership off the ground. But isn't it sad that they wait until people are knocking at their door before they put in the money to do the pub up?

On the wall we created a 240 foot long ceramic mosaic from hundreds of thousands of tiny tiles. It took three years to build, involving and creating 70 jobs, most of which went to the local area. The mosaic has had a lot of publicity, but unfortunately the publicity is mostly interested in whether it's going to get vandalised. That's the question you get all the time. It's a disgrace. If that mosaic was in the centre of a city somewhere, people would be paying to go and see it, because it's an incredible, beautiful work of art. It's re-introducing a sense of beauty to the area, and re-creating a feeling of pride. All the people who live around it don't talk about *the* mosaic any more; they talk about *our* mosaic. Now we can go and knock on the door of the local authority and say, "Look, we've done this. You didn't do it—we did. We want you to do your fair share now and support what we're doing."

Another aspect of what we do is creating paid work. We have set up a community company called Provanhall Holdings and the first thing we did was to create a building company of unemployed craftsmen and tradesmen, and we used whatever money we could get hold of from the Manpower Services Commission, or wherever, to finance it. The company's first job was to take over six empty ground floor houses in an area where, disgracefully, no shops existed—no hairdresser, launderette or solicitor's office, nowhere to get your shoes mended or have a cup of tea—and they turned those empty, unproductive houses into shops, which now provide 30-35 jobs for local people. And it was important to us to create shops with a certain quality, so that people feel they are worth going into. Some shops in Easterhouse never put their metal shutters up and all you want to do is run in and run out again.

Our next project with the building company was to take over an empty school. We knew it was going to close down, so when it was still open we went to the local authority to ask if we could have it to turn into a set of small industrial units for people to work in. The local authority said, "Oh no, we can't do that, but you can try applying for it anyway." It took three years before we eventually got it. The place had been empty for two years and had almost been destroyed. It cost an extra £50,000 to do it up, whereas if they had given it to us the day the school moved out, that money would have been saved. I don't consider that to be imaginative thinking or investment on the part of the local authority.

The school has now been converted into workshop units available for local people to run small businesses from. There are also people there to give help and advice—not people with suits and ties and all that, but people from Easterhouse, who understand what needs to be done. They're there to help people who have a gut feeling about starting a business. Instead of sending them away and saying, "Come back when you've written your business plan," they work with them on the practical details of how to set up that business.

Sadly, the building company couldn't continue after this project because of competition from far better organised firms in Glasgow. However, we intend to start it up again.

We also need to look at a way of getting independent income into the area, as well as stopping the wealth that's there from leaving the area. Maybe, for example, we should set up our own community betting shop in competition to the one that's already there.

People are acting for themselves in Easterhouse and in all the Easterhouses of the world, but that doesn't mean that anyone can sit back and say, "Oh, that's great. They're getting on and doing things for themselves to change their community." They're going to come knocking on your door. They're going to come knocking on the doors of the politicians, of the officials, of government. As they become more confident, people are going to be demanding help. Not charity—but what you have to offer.

In Easterhouse, for example, we live and work in quite an isolated situation. We need contact with others, but we don't have the time or money to pursue it. We no longer have access to telephones, because we can't afford to pay the bills. People can phone in but we can't phone out. We need people to contact us. We need opportunities to share experiences and to know what people have to offer. We need people to work on our behalf in putting these messages across around the world, because this is not the only community where this is going on. And we need money—*some* money. You cannot do something from nothing, which is where we're starting from. The money we receive is put to good use. For example, when the Scottish Development Agency creates one job, it costs them about £5,000. We have created 140 jobs at the cost of £900 a job.

So we are going to come to the people who have the theories, saying, "You've got the theories; we want you to help *us.*" That's a very exciting and challenging thing, and can be quite frightening to a lot of people. But it will happen, and it's happening already. The organisations that are going to be the important ones in the future are those that are going to be able to respond—whether it be the Labour Party, the trade unions, local government bodies or whatever. If they can't respond, local communities are going to ignore them. At the end of the day, they'll be saying, "They can't help us. We're going to do things for ourselves."

Somebody has used the phrase 'on the fringes of the future', and in a way it applies to the sort of work that's going on in Easterhouse. There are no theories at all behind what we do. It comes from a gut feeling that things are wrong, an anger that in Britain, a good Western civilised democratic society, people have to live in conditions that we wouldn't keep animals in. That anger is never, ever going to go away. If it does go away, in fact, then there's absolutely no hope at all for these areas. The work we are doing in Easterhouse and all that we have achieved so far stems from these feelings. At last the community is beginning to write its own plan.

Setting up and Running a Community Business

Linda Ecklin

In an area of Scotland suffering from high levels of unemployment, Linda Ecklin has helped initiate two community businesses—one in her home town of Saltcoats, Ayrshire, and the other a wider-ranging cooperative marketing organisation for home-produced knitwear. She is Vice Chairwoman of Board, TASS Community Enterprises Ltd and in 1984 was awarded a Winston Churchill Fellowship.

I would like to tell you about two community businesses in which I am involved and let you know a bit about what they have done for me personally and for the people involved with them—what they have cost us personally and the benefits we have gained from them.

I live in Saltcoats, a small industrial town of about 15,000 on the west coast of Ayrshire, Scotland. Unemployment in Saltcoats has varied between 25% and 30% for the past few years. In 1981 I and some other people were invited to attend a public meeting about community business. 'Community business' was a phrase I'd never heard before and I knew absolutely nothing about it. However, the meeting was very impressive. The speaker used a lot of words we didn't understand, but the idea of community business sounded good. Work—or lack of it—is a very important issue in working class areas because a person's whole life revolves around having a job and what can be done with the money coming in from it. People don't know any other way to live. This community business idea appeared to be to do with work and creating jobs, even if only on a small scale, so we were very interested.

After that initial public meeting, about half a dozen of us formed a steering committee, and our first six months together were mainly a process of learning what a business was. For instance, we discovered that to start a community business we would have to form a company limited by guarantee, and at first we didn't understand this at all. None of us had ever had anything to do with forming or running a business, so it was all completely foreign—even intimidating. The things involved were things that *other* people had always done, not us. Nonetheless, we wanted to try. So we badgered around, had many a meeting in one another's houses and talked round and round in circles. We had absolutely no money and thought that maybe if we got some, we'd be able to do something. So we managed to acquire an empty shop rent-free for two weeks and had what was really a two-week jumble sale of stuff gathered from various houses in the area. We made £600, which to us was a fortune. "Marks and Spencers, watch yourselves!" we thought.

Meanwhile, we were still attempting to figure out the meaning of phrases like 'limited by guarantee', 'memorandum' and 'articles of a company'. I had spent half my life trying to think of 24 different ways to cook mince, so to begin to think about being a director on the board of a company was something entirely foreign. The idea did hold a certain appeal, however, and when we eventually formed the company and I *did* become a director, I didn't wash the dishes for a week—and there's been no living with me since!

Once we had raised the £600, we looked at the possibilities. There were two ideas that appealed to us, because they didn't need much capital to start them off. One option was to continue to sell second-hand goods. There definitely was a market for that in Saltcoats, especially for children's clothes. The other idea we liked was selling home-produced goods, things people were already making. A lot of people knit, sew, paint or do woodwork. In fact, when you look at the amount of things people can do at home, it is quite exciting, although many of them never see their skill as possibly benefiting themselves and their families by bringing in a little money. So we decided to break into this market and to try to convince people that they had skills which they could use to help their own situation.

In October 1981 we became a limited company—TASS Community Enterprises Ltd. TASS stands for Towns of Ardrossan, Saltcoats and Stevenson. We negotiated to get the empty shop we had used before, but this time paying £100 a month rent on a monthly basis. For about the first six months the shop was staffed entirely voluntarily. We just went in as often as we could and did as much as possible, serving and cleaning. We got quite a lot of coverage on local radio and in the local newspapers. An amazing number of people came into the shop, but it was often funny the way they did it. People are a bit frightened of organisations or anything official. The fact that we were a shop made it easier, but even so they would come in clutching a carrier bag and just look at things. Eventually they would pluck up the courage to say, "I knit," and would pull a jumper out of the bag. This is how most of our home producers came to us. Within a four month period we built up a register of about 120 home producers. We operated on a sale or return basis, with the producer setting the price. We added a ten percent mark-up at that time, which was ludicrous because we weren't even covering the cost of the paper bags we were using. But we've become a bit more commercial since then!

In the meantime, we as a board were putting together an application for Urban Aid funding. Now, this was a death-defying stunt, because we were beginning to discover that the people from whom we could obtain money and aid, such as the Regional Council, spoke a different language from ours. We would go to meetings where they would use expressions like 'sales projections', 'cash flows' and 'business plans', and when we got outside we'd say to each other, "Do *you* know what he meant?" "No, don't *you?*" So it was very difficult for us at first. I would sit trying to remember all these phrases and then phone up the director of the Local Enterprise Advisory Project in the middle of the night asking, "What's a cash flow?" But it was the only way to learn—and we had to learn, because we were realising that in dealing with bodies like the Regional Council you can have the best ideas and all the commitment in the world but if you can't put it all down on paper in the form they want to see it, you're out of the game before you start. We had to learn to do it well—and we did. Our submission for Urban Aid funding took a little time to come through, as these things do, but in October 1983 we received word that we had got funding for three years. There was great jubilation, and vast amounts of personal money were spent on drink and the like. However, we felt we deserved it.

When we first set up the business in the old dilapidated shop, we were turning over maybe £100 a week, out of which we were paying £100 a month rent, a telephone bill and two part-time staff. We were providing an outlet for about 120 local home producers. These people weren't making a lot of money—maybe £6 from a jumper one week— but if you've not got the price of a loaf, £6 is a lot of money. It's the difference between getting to Thursday and not getting to Thursday, which is when the unemployment benefit money comes in. It can be a big difference.

When the Urban Aid funding came through, we opened an

additional shop, also in Saltcoats, called 'Up Market'. The Urban Aid money allowed us to employ a development manager and gave us help with rent and rates and also a small capital sum for shop fittings and suchlike. Our 'Up Market' shop is really a joy to behold; we're so proud of it! It could stand in Princes Street in Edinburgh, no bother—and it is so attractive that it has improved the look of the whole street it is in. It sells only Scottish goods, all hand-crafted, and we are providing an outlet for a lot of craftspeople—and by that I mean people who make a living from their craft—from all over Scotland.

Initially we were a bit afraid that by selling goods from proper crafts-people our own local home producers were going to lose out, that their goods perhaps wouldn't stand up as well. But they are actually selling better. That first shop is turning over about £600 or £700 a week, which for a place like Saltcoats is a lot of money, and is providing an outlet for a large number of people. We still have a lot of work to do though, because we tended to let the old shop stagnate a bit while our attention was on the new one. So we need to bring it up a bit.

The other community business in which I am involved is very different. It's the Home Production Sales Organisation. One of the problems we had in Saltcoats—and it's a problem common to a lot of community businesses, since they are usually set up in areas of very high unemployment—was marketing our goods. We had, for instance, a man who was producing beautiful inlaid woodwork tobacco bowls and fruit bowls. Well, when you've not got any money, you're not really interested in buying a beautiful wooden tobacco bowl; that's the least of your worries. So we realised that we needed to get a market outside our area for these things. Other community businesses were having the same problem, so about three years ago a group of us from all the different areas in the central belt of Scotland began to meet under the guidance of the director of the Local Enterprise Advisory Project. We found we were all hitting the same problems at one time or another, so we shared information and tried to learn from each others' mistakes. In tackling the problem of finding a market for our goods, we came up with the idea of a home production sales organisation which would look for markets for the best of what was being produced in each area. We tried various ways of doing this, but without success. We spent a lot of time trying to produce a catalogue, but problems arose. For example, the man at our end who was producing the beautiful woodwork was making these things in his kitchen at home. If we found a buyer and they wanted even as little as ten tobacco bowls in the next two months, they could forget it. Production was very, very slow. The man also liked to make whatever he wanted to make. He didn't want to make ten tobacco bowls; he wanted to make one tobacco bowl, then an ash-tray, then a fruit bowl. The man was quite happy doing that, so *that* was fine: but it was very difficult to look for a market while production was on that level.

We spent a lot of time and effort on this, but it wasn't going to work. So we looked again at what we were doing and thought that maybe if there was a skill we all had in common, we could try marketing that particular one. There was such a skill, and it was knitting. There were women knitting all over the place. So we looked at the knitwear trade and felt that traditional knitwear—Aran, Fairisle, Icelandic and Shetland—was fairly well covered. A lot of companies are doing it well and efficiently, and they have a market. We wondered whether we really wanted to start competing in that game. I had a strong notion to get into high fashion knitwear. Now, the fashion industry is fiercely competitive; a lot of the people involved are absolutely deadly and desperate. Nonetheless, fashion changes all the time, so if you just happen to be doing the right thing at the right time, you've got a market. Since nobody else had a better idea, this is what we did.

The first step was to get some designs, and I volunteered to do them. I hadn't a clue at first, and I wondered how on earth I was going to do it, especially with four children, three cats and two dogs under my feet! Anyway, we came up with some designs and showed them at the Scottish Trade Fair at Ingliston, and came home with £3,000 worth of orders. This time I didn't do the dishes for *two* weeks! It was a wonderful morale boost to the people involved. We were totally beside ourselves. We had gone to the Trade Fair not really sure of what to expect. We felt like just staying in a corner so that nobody would notice us, but suddenly there were these people saying,"Oh, this is wonderful." We weren't really sure if it was us they were talking to.

So the Home Production Sales Organisation sallied forth into the fashion world. We exhibited at Ingliston again the following year, and we've had quite a lot of interest from the United States, the Middle East, Canada and Germany. Last year I visited the USA and now we have two agents in New York who want to work for us out there, which makes us sound terribly international!

How this particular community business will go from here, I'm not quite clear. We've got a lot to do. Coming up with designs is difficult. It's also quite difficult for us to balance what we feel we can pay the knitters with the cost of yarn and all our other expenses, and still end up with a reasonable price on the garment. If we don't sell our goods, then we're not going to have work for anybody. And pulling the knitters together can be quite a problem, because most of the women who knit for us only do it when they feel like it—we got the most knitting done when the Olympics were on, because they were sitting up all night watching TV. But it's very difficult to impress on them that when we get an order there's a delivery deadline.

Buyers, you see, don't want to know about your ideals. In fact, frequently I don't even mention what kind of business we are. As far as they're concerned, we're just another knitwear company. They're no more interested in our ideals than flying in the air. The fact that we pay our knitters better, that they are heavily involved in what we are doing, that two of the knitters are on the board of the company, and that we're trying to work differently from the traditional way—all that is irrelevant to the buyers. We are going to stand or fold on what they see on the hanger—nothing more and nothing less.

So on the one hand, we have to be commercial—but on the other, we are trying to balance that against all the things we want to change in the way we work. What we are really doing is working with a new idea with all sorts of social implications, but within a very traditional system, and right now what we are doing is working the system to suit us. It's hard to do sometimes, but we're trying—and we've got a lot going for us.

For instance, although our operation is small, it's very adaptable. All our sweaters are hand-knit, so it's all very controllable and easily changed: you can never knit more than one thing at a time on one pair of needles. Then also there are a lot of knowledgeable people in organisations like the Scottish Development Agency and the local Enterprise Advisory Project—and also hard-line commercial people—who are very willing to help us with things we don't know about. And of course there are more community businesses in existence now than there were four years ago, so the network is better, and we can support and learn from one another.

Community Businesses:
Every Community Should Have One

John Pearce

John Pearce is Director of the Local Enterprise Advisory Project, Strathclyde Community Business, an organisation which provides a variety of support and backup for local initiatives towards relieving problems of unemployment in some of the most economically depressed areas of Scotland.

The community business movement in central Scotland has grown out of the initiatives of local people in some of the most economically depressed areas. In four communities in particular—Govan, Easterhouse, Port Glasgow and Ferguslie Park—there were the stirrings in 1977 or 1978 of what has since become the community business movement throughout central Scotland.

Govan is a shipbuilding area of Glasgow which has been in decline for some years. Back in 1977 a community anti-poverty project, funded by the European Community, the Gulbenkian Foundation and others, was set up to look at problems in that area and to try to find ways in which local people could do something about them. Quite clearly, one of the problems was the decline of the economy and the growing rate of unemployment, so a group of local people who shared that concern were brought together to discuss possible solutions. One of the group's members was an elderly woman who put forward an idea she had heard about on a TV programme which involved taking a redundant building and converting it into small workshops. This idea had been tried out in parts of England but never in Scotland, and the working party discussed the possibility of their undertaking something similar in Govan.

We have heard from Chris Elphick of the Easterhouse Festival Society how at about the same time some people from that housing estate were looking at their community and recognising that something had to be done to create a local economy both to provide services and commercial activity and to prevent the enormous economic leakages that were taking place as people spent their money outside the community. Meanwhile, in Port Glasgow, a group of community workers, also concerned about the decline of shipbuilding, were beginning to wonder what form of response they should make to their own problems of a declining local economy and rising unemployment. And in Ferguslie Park, one of most notorious housing estates in the west of Scotland, some tenants were trying to find a way to start creating work in the community. Ferguslie Park is one of those very sad communities where people with far-reaching difficulties were clustered together by the housing authorities during the 50s and 60s. Such communities not only have very high rates of unemployment—up to four times the national average—but they also suffer from a multiplicity of community and social problems. In the 70s some tenants of Ferguslie Park had tried to set up a small workers' cooperative in joinery, using funds from the Manpower Services Commission, but this had failed. Nevertheless, they were still searching for a way in which they as a community could start creating real jobs rather than the dead-end short-term jobs generally funded by the MSC. They were interested in real work and not make-work.

The community business movement which began stirring in these four communities in 1977 and 1978 has two important foundations. Firstly, it has arisen from local people asking, "What can *we* do? What action can we take to tackle unemployment and the declining economy in our communities rather than wait for others, whether the public or private sector, to do it for us?" Secondly, it is based on a tradition of community action which over the years has tackled problems of housing, care of the elderly and recreational space. That experience has been translated and applied to the unemployment problem. Quite clearly, the issue of unemployment and the local economy has become the key question for many communities.

Some exciting projects have emerged over the past five or six years in those four communities and I will mention them briefly before looking at their more theoretical implications. In Govan, the employment study group eventually created a company called Govan Workspace Ltd and acquired from the Regional Council a disused primary school which has been converted into 37 small workshops. Govan Workspace is community owned and based, and is pledged to plough its profits back into the local community both by improving the business and by supporting other related projects. In addition to acquiring the school, they have since then negotiated with the Scottish Development Agency to take over a disused factory which will provide another 50 workshops. The workshops they create are purposely small, ranging from 250 sq ft upwards. When the project was first discussed, the Scottish Development Agency considered 'small' as being about 5,000 sq ft, but they have learned a lot over the past few years, partly because groups like Govan Workspace have been pushing the case for small workshops as one appropriate way of helping revive a local economy. To sum up the company's achievement, they have created 100,000 sq ft of workshop space which will have brought 350 or more jobs into the local area; as a company they employ six people directly; they have brought over £1½ million of investment into that depressed part of Glasgow; and they have also created two other small businesses out of their activities—a printing business and a snack food packaging and distribution company.

It is easy to list all that in a few seconds and to make it sound a simple story of success. In fact, along the way there have been enormous problems. One of the biggest of these has been convincing official bodies like the Regional Council and the Scottish Development Agency that a group of ordinary local folk have the capacity to handle a project like this. This problem of credibility lingers on, because the public sector is by no means convinced that community-based enterprises can function successfully as fairly large businesses. There are, however, two particularly inspiring aspects of the Govan project which I want to emphasise. First, Govan Workspace are reaching the stage where they can support other projects; at a very exciting company seminar earlier this year they began to look ahead at how they could use the profit they know they are going to make to create new employment opportunities in the locality. Secondly, the same group of people who originally sat around the table all those years ago—with the exception of the woman who first had the idea, because sadly she died—are now running the company as its directors.

In Easterhouse the group's initiative has led to the conversion of six houses into shops in a very depressed part of the community; they have acquired a disused school and converted it into workshops; their company, Provanhall Holdings, is planning to set up a building business based on the people who took part in converting the houses and the school; and they are now looking for ways of acquiring other buildings in the area to help stimulate more business activities. An exciting aspect of their work is their plan to look at the economy of Easterhouse as a whole and find ways in which they as a community-based company can begin to plug some of the leakages in the community's wealth.

In Port Glasgow, as a result of the community workers wondering what to do about unemployment, a group of local people came together and set up a business called Port Glasgow Community Enterprises Ltd, which has become a holding company for three separate projects. One is Inverclyde Crafts, which specialises in knitwear and sells its goods throughout the UK and abroad. They have 120 home knitters on their books—women who are supplementing a very slender family income by doing some knitting in their free time. The second company, called Inverclyde Goodwill and based on a very successful American model, takes cast-off furniture from the better-off, refurbishes it and then sells it to people who are looking for good quality second-hand furniture. The third company has developed out of that recycling operation: Inverclyde Furnishings re-upholsters furniture and is about to go into furniture manufacturing. These three companies employ about 20 people between them at present.

The tenants' association in Ferguslie Park, with a very energetic vice-chairman who once worked as a stone-cleaner, put together a plan to create a stone-cleaning and restoration business. It was initially set up with funding from the Manpower Services Commission to clean graffiti off public buildings, and later made a slow and somewhat difficult transition into a fully commercial business employing up to 35 people at peak times. They are now looking at where they should go from here as a company and how they should expand their base of activities.

There are now some 35 community businesses in central Scotland, and there are as many again in the planning stages. The concept of community business has finally acquired a certain seal of approval from the authorities: in the Strathclyde region an agency called Strathclyde Community Business Ltd, for which I work, has been set up with the backing of the Regional Council, the SDA, the district councils, the private sector and the community business movement itself; in the Central region there is a development unit called Community Business Central, which has the backing of the Regional Council and the Urban Programme; and in the Lothian Region, Community Business Lothian has recently acquired its first employee. These units have been set up to help people do something themselves about unemployment and economic problems in areas where unemployment rates can be as high as 50% or 60% of the adult population, and where young people face almost no prospects for employment in the immediate future. Serving the whole of Scotland is Community Business Scotland, a federal organisation which links together a network of people, organisations and initiatives and provides information and backup support.

A community business is a mechanism for stimulating and reviving local economic activity. During the past two years of our work within Strathclyde we have been describing it as a strategy which reaches areas other strategies cannot reach. A community business has a number of particular characteristics. Firstly, it is community owned and usually based on a certain neighbourhood or locality. Secondly, it is non-profit-distributing. In other words, the directors are lay directors; they are not in it to make a profit for themselves, but to make a surplus which can be reinvested in the locality. Thirdly, it is limited by guarantee and in some cases acquires charitable status. Fourthly, it is very often multi-functional, in that more than one business activity is carried on within it.

The important factor and the reason why community businesses are usually targeted at the areas of highest unemployment is that they are about creating a local economic infrastructure in areas where none exists. It is in places like Easterhouse, considered to have no economy in the normal sense of the word, that community businesses can provide a structure for creating economic activity, organising work, attracting resources into the community and providing management and other skills needed by groups and individuals who want to set up their own enterprises.

Ideally, a community business could be involved in six different areas of activity. Firstly, it will be creating viable, profitable businesses in order to provide jobs and to make a profit—nothing exceptional about that. Secondly, it will also be running what can best be described as marginal enterprises which can also create jobs for local people and/or provide an important service for the locality. Thirdly, it will be providing resources for local people to plan and develop their own enterprises. We must recognise that in many areas of high unemployment, traditional attitudes are such that most people find it hard to conceive of anything other than working for somebody else; that they might begin to do something on their own account, either individually or in partnership with others, is a new concept to them. It is important, therefore, to offer assistance to people in moving towards this independence, which means providing premises, advice, various management and guidance services, hand-holding and perhaps even a legal structure under which they can take their first tentative steps.

Fourthly, a community business will take action to save or safeguard local jobs. A company can take action quickly, but if that structure doesn't exist, precious days, weeks and months can be lost in creating it, by which time the moment has passed and the action missed. Fifthly, a community business can sponsor MSC-type schemes for community benefit but, whereas the Manpower Services Commission handles the short-term make-work type of job opportunities which have the effect of reducing unemployment numbers by a small amount and doing little else, a community business can make sure that these projects develop into more commercial and viable enterprises. Finally, a community business can organise local community services on a sub-contract basis from the public authorities.

The slogan of the community business movement for the next decade should be 'Every community should have one', because those businesses are a means both of stimulating and encouraging economic activity and thus the creation of wealth, and of mixing economic objectives with social and community objectives. This blend of the social and the commercial, the community and the business, is distinctive of community business—and the very thing, of course, that others often find hardest to accept. A few years ago we approached a major bank for assistance with one particular project and they replied with what, in my view, has become a classic letter. I paraphrase it here: "What you describe is not really a business, which could be considered by our usual small business loans scheme, but yet it is too commercial to be considered by our community support programme, which is aimed mainly at charities."

I recently attended a conference which brought together various sections of the new cooperative movement—community businesses, workers' co-ops, housing co-ops and credit unions—and I was struck by some of the early definitions of cooperation. In 1659, for instance, a man called Peter Cornelius Plockhoy, a Dutchman living in London, wrote a pamphlet in which he outlined a scheme for setting up cooperative businesses. The full title of his pamphlet was: "A way propounded to make the poor in these and other nations happy by bringing together a fit, suitable and well-qualified people unto one household government, or little commonwealth, wherein everyone may keep his propriety and be employed in some work or other as he shall be fit, without being oppressed; being the way not only to rid this and other nations from idle, evil and disorderly persons but also from all such that have sought and found out many inventions to live upon the labour of others." Plockhoy went on to describe how all profits would be used for the common good, in order "to eschew the yoke of the temporal and spiritual pharaohs who have long enough domineered over our bodies and souls". Housing would be provided for the members, education for both children and adults, welfare for the retired and a health service for all.

Then there was Robert Owen, of course, who tried to put his vision of a working cooperative community into practice in New Lanark early in the 19th century, and who, in his third deed of partnership made in 1813, states that all profits made in the concern beyond 5% per annum on capital invested should be laid aside for the benefit of the workers and the community at large.

There were also the Rochdale pioneers who opened their historic store in Lancashire in 1844. They intended to build a cooperative community involved not only in retail but also in manufacture, agriculture, education and housing. Their objectives were very clear and specific: "The establishment of a store for the sale of provisions, clothing etc; the building, purchasing or erecting of a number of houses in which those members desiring to assist each other in improving their domestic and social conditions may reside; to commence the manufacture of articles for the employment of members as may be without employment or who may be suffering as a consequence of repeated reductions in their wages. The society shall purchase or rent an estate or estates of land which shall be cultivated by the members who may be out of employment or whose labour may be badly remunerated; and as soon as practicable this society shall proceed to arrange the powers of production, distribution, education."

In all these examples there is the notion of people working together to help themselves, each other and the wider community, striking a balance between self and other, between personal gain and community gain. Three important themes relevant to community business emerge from these definitions. Firstly, there is the concept of community gain. It seems to me that community and cooperative enterprises are not just about self-benefit but about self-benefit within the context of benefit for the wider community, which means that a system has to be devised whereby community gain can be assessed alongside benefit to individuals. Profitability and efficiency are essential but they are only the means to an end. The purpose of the enterprise is to benefit its members and the community.

The second important theme is social auditing and accounting.

If cooperative and community enterprises are to have social and community objectives as well as commercial ones, it is important to find ways of measuring to what extent these are achieved. Just as business plans are important projections against which to chart the actual performance of a business, so it is important to establish a plan of social benefit objectives in order to measure achievement, although that can often be difficult to do.

However, social auditing and accounting goes far beyond simply planning for social benefit and measuring achievement; it is also a process of balancing financial profit and loss with social benefit and non-benefit. The annual balance sheet of a cooperative enterprise or community business should take into account the fact that costs are incurred in meeting social and community benefits, but also that those benefits can represent savings and other advantages to the cooperative community, the wider community and indeed the state. In looking at the annual accounts of Govan Workspace recently, I noticed that on the income side there was a grant of £30,000 from the Regional Council which they still receive to help them through their buildup years, but I also noticed on the other side that the company is now paying rates—or causing rates to be paid—to the local authority in the amount of £33,000 per annum. What is received is immediately given back, and that's without allowing for all the other payments back to the state—in the form of taxes, national insurance contributions and so on—as a result of the work Govan Workspace has done. It is absolutely essential to balance the financial assistance provided to help a community cooperative or business get going in an area of high unemployment against savings in paying out long-term unemployment benefit, in tax and national insurance contributions being paid in, in increased circulation of money in the area generally and, perhaps, in less clients for the social services, the health services and the police.

These twin concepts of community gain and social accounting are, it seems to me, essential ingredients of the new cooperative movement, of which I see community businesses as an important part. It is on those two concepts particularly that we have to construct an argument in favour of positive discrimination towards this type of enterprise within communities where there remains no economy worth talking about.

The third theme that emerges from the examples I gave is that cooperation is envisaged as touching all aspects of life—trade and commerce, distribution, manufacturing, agriculture, housing, education, saving, lending, insurance and so on. This interlinking of various aspects of our economic life with aspects of our social and community life is central to the concept of community business, and is very important, I believe, for the future operation of our society. For too long we have maintained a separation between work and home, between the economic and the social. At the conference I referred to earlier we discussed ways in which community businesses could help set up schemes like credit unions, how housing cooperatives could put their work out to workers' cooperatives and community businesses and how community businesses could encourage groups they were working with to form workers' co-ops. That's just a start. We need to explore more widely the interaction of various aspects of economic and social life and to count gain in a context of general benefit rather than simple financial profit to a narrow group. This is what the community business movement is all about.

Part IV

Perspectives on a World Economy

Choices and Necessities

Peter Schwartz

*Peter Schwartz, from the USA, is chief planning officer with Royal
Dutch Shell International in London and co-author (with Paul Hawken
and Jay Ogilvy) of* **Seven Tomorrows: Toward a Voluntary
History**.

NOW UNTIL TOMORROW
CAN BE A LONG-LONG TIME
OF MIND

What I want to do is present a view of the world economy—how it's
working and why, and where it may be going—as seen from the
perspective of a very large company. Shell is, in fact, the second largest
company in the world, although it is organised in an extremely
decentralised manner. But let me hasten to add that I speak for myself
and not for Shell. My views are not necessarily shared by everyone
within the company, although they are by some. Of course, my views
influence Shell and are part of the mindset and view of the world that
informs the company's decisions, since my job is to lead a small group
who make an ongoing indepth study of the world today—including
how its economy, political systems, energy, technology and social
change are all interacting to create the daily life around us and that of
the decades ahead—in order that the decision-makers of Shell can make
better decisions about the future of the company. So the view I present
here is one that in part arises out of the analysis my team and I have
performed over the course of several years.

First of all, I will set out what I take to be certain basic assumptions
about how the world works. Secondly, I'll try to suggest a framework
for thinking about the future of the world economy. Thirdly, I'll look
at some of the forces shaping that future. And finally, I'll conclude
with some thoughts about how it may all work out and what we can do
about it.

I am not an economist, but I am going to put forward certain views
on economics and some people who may be more rigorous economists

than I will perhaps wish to challenge them. In dealing with basic assumptions I want to touch on two levels—sacred and secular. It is important, I feel, in talking about something like economics to put it in a sacred context. I was raised as a fairly religious Jew and, although in many ways that is behind me, it is also still very much part of me. I have also been a student of Tibetan and Zen Buddhism for many years. But perhaps much more important than that have been a few very personal experiences that have shaped my view of how the world works and of what lies behind its outer reality. Some of those experiences have occurred in places of profound loneliness and beauty, such as while backpacking with my wife in the High Sierras. Others have taken place in much more mundane settings, like the kitchen of a house I lived in in Ruislip just outside London in 1966. But uniting all those experiences is one simple conclusion: that the universe is a very, very mysterious place. When anyone tells me they know what the nature of things is or what God is, I do not believe them. The only thing I can be sure of is that I don't know; that's the one certainty in my life. In those special moments I was able to grasp only that there is something much vaster, deeper and more enduring, but my mind and spirit were simply incapable of comprehending its ultimate nature. This is part of the human condition—something that inevitably leads us to accept a profound humility about what we can know and what is knowable. And it is that which leads me to a less sacred perspective, because the lesson learned at the sacred level has only been reinforced in more secular realms.

I used to be an aeronautical engineer and one of the things that emerged from my studies—which included nuclear and astro-physics and mathematics in its highest form—was again that we honestly don't know anything. I was very much struck by the fact that in the late 19th century an American committee of physicists reached the conclusion that by the end of the 19th century most of the basic mysteries of reality would have been solved and there would be an oversupply of physicists because there wouldn't be any problems left to work on. It didn't quite work out that way, of course, and today most physicists would probably agree that we are much less sure about the nature of things than we were at the end of the 19th century. I suspect physicists at the end of the 21st century and the 25th century may be saying the same thing. It is our hubris to imagine we are simply one step from ultimate reality and that only a few more years from now we will suddenly achieve it. From my experience in the sciences I have concluded that essentially there is a long way to go; we are just a short way into that process of learning.

My involvement with economics and politics has also given me some perspectives on how the world works. One person in particular has influenced me in this respect and that is Jay Ogilvy, one of the people who co-authored *Seven Tomorrows* with me. In his book *Many Dimensional Man* Jay develops the concept of what he calls neo-nature. His idea is that when humans were much more primitive they lived in an environment consisting basically of two kinds of elements—nature and other people. To cope with these elements tools were developed: technology to cope with nature and politics to cope with other people. At that simple level these were in humanity's control: they made their tools with their own hands, so they understood how they came into existence and how to fix them when they broke; and politics was at the village level and thus simple to organise. What has happened over time, however, is that our tools have become our environment. We no longer understand them or how they work. Very few people, for example, know how to fix a car. Most of us don't know the nature of the technology that surrounds us, nor do we understand the organisations we participate in, and we certainly don't control them. This lack of understanding and loss of control is fundamental to the condition of modern societies, and it is because our tools have become a new natural environment that we speak of moods and climates. We talk, for example, about the economic climate, and indeed controlling the economy is just about as impossible as controlling the weather, while the art of economic forecasting is in fact much less reliable than the art of weather forecasting.

This new kind of environment in turn affects our concept of power. It is important to be very clear about what we mean in this respect. Power is the capacity to realise your intentions, to get done what you want done. There is an important distinction between power and force: force knocks things over; power allows you to build something. It's a crucial difference. In the new natural environment of very complex organisations working with sophisticated technologies, it is very difficult to exert real and meaningful power to get things accomplished. Remember those big pipe organs they have in old churches? When the organ master plays the instrument, a harmonious sound comes out. The problem with modern civilisation and its organisations is that the keys are connected in so many complex and different ways that when you press them you get unexpected sounds—and more often than not you produce a cacophony rather than harmony. The task therefore is to establish linkages between intentions and outcomes. These are very diffuse indeed; very few policy-makers in the modern environment get the outcome they intend. There is no better example than the arms race. Both sides are arming themselves furiously to increase their own security, but what they are actually doing is diminishing the security of us all. Another example of this can be seen in Mr Reagan's attempts to solve the problems of the American economy; he has simply substituted one set of problems with another set. This is all most of our policies do, in fact.

Such complexity in our systems produces a phenomenon for which in France they have a wonderful phrase—'perverse effect', meaning the opposite effect of what was intended. A good example of this was the attempt by the Cultural Minister of France to save small bookstores which were being destroyed by the large discount stores. To correct the situation he banned discounts so that all stores could compete equally. The consequence, however, was that the big stores, being that much more efficient and now charging full price, made even more profit—and with that profit they bought up the small bookstores, thus hastening their decline. A perverse effect also resulted from the urban housing programmes of the 60s in the US, which were intended to improve the amount and quality of housing for the poor. The net result, however, was lower quality housing and less of it. So it is very important to understand what we mean by power in the context of this new kind of environment.

The fundamental conclusion I come to in economics is that markets work. You can play around with them, you can change the rules, but they always work; people will follow the nature of the market. This leads me to propose that perhaps the most powerful conservation organisation on earth is not Friends of the Earth, although I support what they do, nor the Sierra Club, of which I am a long-standing member, but OPEC. OPEC has done more for conservation than anyone else. They did not intend to, of course—in fact their motive was self-interest—but nonetheless the outcome was conservation. We use much less oil today and we are going to use less resources of all kinds because OPEC in their greed raised the price of oil. This is the conservation effect of the market place. However, the bottom line is that we do not know what will happen in the future. Because of the complexity underlying response to markets the situation is fundamentally unpredictable. To anyone who maintains they know what is going to happen in the future of economics I would quote two ancient proverbs, one Chinese and the other Arab. The Arab one says: "He who predicts the future lies even if he tells the truth." The Chinese one is: "He who lives by the crystal ball will die from eating broken glass."

Another basic assumption I make is that economics is fundamentally situational. Economists have sought to treat it as if it were something with iron laws that endure for all time. There may be such laws in nature—I'm not even sure about that—but I am sure there are no such laws in economics. The only constant in the world is change, and as a result economics must always be situational, in terms of both place and time. The economic system of a village in Argentina or Africa is not the same as that of a village in Scotland, and the economics of a village anywhere are not the same as the economics of a country, which in turn differ from those of the world as a whole. Again, the economics of a business or industry are not the same as those of a variety of other situations. Furthermore, economics changes over time. The economics of the 1950s are not those of the 80s, and those of the 80s will not be those of 2010. The world changes and the rules of the game evolve.

We have to deal also with some fundamental moral questions: What is right action? What is appropriate in various situations? As a conscientious objector to the Vietnam war I was very much involved in the anti-war movement and so these questions have plagued me for years. The one overwhelming conclusion I have come to—and the OPEC case makes the point very well— is that what matters is morality of outcome, not morality of intention. What we wish to have happen is by and large irrelevant. What we actually do and the effect we have on the world is what counts, but it is a much harder thing to pinpoint. It's fairly easy to know what one wants. It's much harder to predict what will actually happen as a result of one's actions. There are endless examples of good intentions producing tragic outcomes. I stood against the Vietnam war and I still think it was right to do so. However, if the fall of Cambodia and the holocaust that resulted there was part of the consequence of that decision, I have profound doubts that will always remain with me. Millions of people died in Cambodia and one of the reasons for that may have been the outcome of the Vietnam war; I don't know and I will always remain unsure. So these are not easy questions—and they are very real questions. But I do know that it is what actually happens that counts.

A Jungian therapist called Erich Neumann raised a difficult question at the end of the last war in a book called *Depth Psychology and a New*

130

Ethic. He pointed out that it was human beings who had created World War II, who had bombed Dresden and Hiroshima and built Auschwitz and Treblinka. Those things weren't done by creatures from another planet; the capacity for them exists in the human psyche. What conclusions can we draw from this for right action? His conclusion—and one I share—is that human beings are extremely complex, and simple mechanical models of the way the human mind works are entirely inadequate. Neumann likened the mind of the individual to a kind of psychological league of nations in which many kinds of personalities and characters are represented, all fighting for a place; and one way or another they will be heard. What is required therefore is to provide a forum for those different subpersonalities within each of us, so that we attain a sense of balance. That sense of balance is extremely important. If one approaches life with a sense of mystery and unknowingness, then one must always question any inner perspective and every moral judgment.

In looking to the future, two people have said things that have particularly influenced me. Goethe said: "Whatever you can do or dream you can, begin it. Boldness has genius, power and magic in it." It is important to be bold and to be willing to dream. On the other hand, Dick Raymond, the founder of the Portola Institute, said: "If it doesn't take 50 years, it isn't worth doing." This also is an important perspective, because our ego wishes to accomplish things in our own lifetime and see the rewards quickly. I was very impressed when I visited the Gaudi cathedral being built in Barcelona. Designed in the early 1920s, it will be finished only in something like 100 or 150 years from now. As they raise money, more gets built; as the money runs out, less work is done. I met a young stonecutter there, whose father had worked on the cathedral. He was gone now; the son himself might see the roof put on, and maybe his children will see the front facade, but he will never see the cathedral's completion. No-one who enters that building 300 years from now will know the name of this stonecutter, but his legacy will be enduring. He knows that what really endures takes a long time to create.

All these basic assumptions leave me feeling very humble in the face of the deep mysteries and unpredictability of the real world, so take what I'm about to say concerning the future of the world economy with a grain of salt, because I don't know whether it's right. As a framework, I tend to think of economics in terms of biological evolution, not at all as a mechanical system. It is a system evolving over time

131

and, as in biology, theory has changed. The Darwinian model of evolution we were taught at school was essentially one of gradual mutation through interbreeding: over time new capabilities emerge which are tested in the battle for survival, and out of that battle new species are born and old ones die. This rarely happens, however. We have discovered from geological records that more often than not something quite different occurs. It seems that from time to time there are moments of profound change, when the basic conditions of life alter and many species die and others are born all at once within the space of a few thousand years. In between are equilibrium phases, long periods of relative balance and stability, when things change only slowly. The moments of change come suddenly, such as when the climate became colder and the dinosaurs died out within a few thousand years.

I have often imagined the last dinosaur wandering in a swamp as the mud slowly froze around its legs, looking around rather stupidly and wondering when things were going to get back to normal. Most economists are a bit like that too. Well, things are not going to get back to normal; they never do. In economics we go through similar phases—long periods of expansion and growth of the sort we had from the 50s through the 60s, alternating with periods of change and transition, often punctuated by shocks, such as the breakdown of the monetary order in 1971, the oil shock, the debt shock, and now maybe the dollar shock. These phases of economic development are very important because the rules differ from one to the other. During the expansion phases the emphasis is on more, bigger and better of the same; essentially it is quantitative change that rules. In periods of transition like the present it is qualitative change that matters—changes in kind and in the basic rules of the game.

The present period of transition will eventually give way to a new period of expansion in five, ten or fifteen years, depending on how we play the game and what options are open to us. But there are two other fundamental principles involved in the process of transition that are important to keep in mind, and they have been put forward by two different economists, Mancur Olson in the United States and Joseph Schumpeter from Austria. Olson, in his book *The Rise and Decline of Nations*, talks about the silting of the stream, comparing an economy to a river whose flow changes over time. What happens is that the people who gain from the success of one period try to protect the *status quo* by erecting barriers. They fight to hold on to what they have won—but they can't win in the end because nature always wins; evolution continues and the rules of one phase break down. These people can hang on for a hell of a long time, however, and make life pretty miserable for themselves and others. The stream must be cleared of silt before it can flow on.

A very similar process, described by Schumpeter, is that of creative destruction, meaning that old things must die for new ones to be born. In economics we have a very hard time facing the idea of death, but it is one of the inevitabilities of life, as true for nations, big industries and small businesses as it is for individual people. Things grow and decline—and it is important to recognise that this is a natural process which cannot be halted but can in fact be managed either more or less painfully. Among the societies best at managing this process of creative destruction is Japan. They have learned how to ease the pain that the destructive forces cause both for people and companies, but they move on. They have moved from iron, steel and shipbuilding to automobiles, biotechnology and electronics; but the point is they keep moving on, whereas societies like the UK are very resistant to the process of change.

I want now to speculate a little about the various forces creating the longer-term future. First, and among the most powerful, is one that surprised nearly everyone, myself included. It is the power of affluence. Back in the 1950s two books published in the US, called *The Organisation Man* and *The Man in the Grey Flannel Suit*, put forward the idea that as we became richer we would all become the same. The whole world was going to look like Los Angeles, God help us. But it didn't turn out that way; in fact, the richer we became, the more diverse we became. As we grew more affluent and found we had more options, our innate psychological differences found room for expression and more and more variety began to appear in basic values and lifestyles. This is, I feel, an extremely important perspective to keep in mind, because it means that no single lifestyle is seen as the one true way of living or will come to dominate the world or any region of it. The more people develop and grow, the more diverse they will become. There may be a fundamental unity behind all human existence but it will not be expressed in our day to day life.

That diversity must make us humble again in what we can expect to accomplish by way of political change, because it will be reflected in different views in politics and economics. People will have different aspirations, different judgments of what is right and wrong, and of what the future ought to be. One of our greatest challenges, therefore, is managing the inevitability of conflict in a diverse world. Conflict can be destructive or it can be creative. We can draw enormous richness from diversity. My staff consists of people of twelve different nationalities and it isn't always peaceful; we have huge fights and some of them have their roots in our national and cultural differences. Part of my job is to be a conflict manager among some very bright people who are all very sure of what they know based on whichever culture they come from; but it's worth the struggle because of the richness of the views that emerge.

The second important force is the growth of human potential. In economics the growth of gross national product results from increase in labour force plus increase in productivity, and both of these depend on people. Thus, growth in human potential can mean a greater number of people; but it can also mean more able people. We are seeing more and more better educated and healthier people in much of the world, although not in all of it—in some places, especially Africa, the outlook is very dire indeed. But in some other areas the prospects are remarkable. In the early 60s it was predicted that India would be starving to death by now, but that hasn't happened. Although the progress is not what many would have wished or hoped for, it is nevertheless a remarkable achievement and India by no means has mass starvation.

In Shell we have done a study of indicators of social and economic development, and contrary to the dominant view that economic development precedes social development—in other words, you have to get rich before you can take care of your people—we have found it is a mutual process: that if you improve the quality of people's life, they will be much more successful economic actors, meaning they will start businesses and be more productive workers, more able citizens and better informed in terms of how the world works. Therefore investments in education and health are investments in economic development—a first and necessary step towards the future of economic growth for the world.

A third major force moving us towards the future is the growth of technology. Like it or not, technology proceeds and our capabilities continue to grow, some of them destructive and some remarkably creative. Every once in a while in human history a major new technology comes along that changes everything. The last one was the internal combustion engine, which increased the possibilities of mobility. Now, with the development of micro-electronics, we have distributed intelligence. Forget about computers; think in terms of highly intelligent machines. In the next 20 to 30 years every machine on earth will

134

become much more intelligent because of micro-electronics. This means that services will become high-technology, and that capital-intensive businesses and the world in general will become much more efficient, which is one of the main reasons we in Shell think oil demand is going to go down rather than up. For example, I recently visited Amory Lovins' house in Colorado. In his house he has a light switch containing a little microprocessor attached to a photo cell and infrared detector. All you have to do is set the light level you want in the room and, as the sun moves across the sky during the day and the clouds shift, the microprocessor automatically adjusts the brightness of the light to maintain it at the required level. The infrared detector can tell whether you are in the room or not and turns the light on when you come in and off when you leave. The net saving of this system is 90%; it uses only 10% of the energy the previous system did. The whole switch costs only $30 and it takes seven months to pay for itself. Another example of the impact of micro-electronics comes from the Ford Motor Company, which in a recent study worked out that as a result of new technology the average American car in the year 2000 will give 100 miles per gallon, compared with an average of 20-25 to-day. Both of these are examples of an enormous increase in efficiency made possible by developments in technology—and we owe that to OPEC. Because they raised the price of oil, suddenly it became interesting to design efficient automobiles and new kinds of light switches.

The fourth major force for the future is the growing interdependence of the various parts of the world, and the tension between the need for such interdependence and the desire for independence. One of the dominant features of the postwar era was the end of colonialism and the rise of independent countries. When the UN was founded in 1947 it consisted of only about 50 countries; today there are 170. During the 70s one of the dominant trends was the growth of *inter*dependence, particularly because of an increase in financial relationships so enormous that last year world financial flows totalled $30 trillion, ten times the US gross national product. All that money is flowing around the world uncontrolled. Most of it was fed originally from the industrialised world to OPEC, whereupon it was put back in the banks and then handed out to the LDCs (lesser developed countries) in what was probably the largest unintentional foreign aid programme ever created, because of course most of that debt will never be repaid. We distinguish between 'polite' defaults and 'impolite' defaults. Everybody so far has engaged in polite defaults—that's when you don't pay but you say you will. The important point is that through the growth of phenomena like the interdependence of the world economy, individual nations and companies have lost the control they once thought they had over the system as a whole. The system has become so complex that their leverage on it has become very weak.

A characteristic of complex systems is that they are very resilient. One of the surprises of the past few years is that the world economic system hasn't broken down, especially with events like the defaults of Mexico, Brazil and Argentina and the great recession that has occurred. The fact that the system survived through all this indicates the extent of its resilience. I call it resilient fragility; it looks like it's going to break all the time but it never quite does. However, this characteristic also makes the system difficult to change. If a breakdown of any kind is going to occur, the most likely form it will take will not, I feel, be war but a real division. Diversity, as I mentioned before, is very much a condition of the world. One of the most striking examples is the different ways the Russians and the Americans see the world—and I don't think it's ideological; ideology is just an excuse in the East-West race. It has always been a fact in history that two great empires get at each other and they will always find some good reason to do so. Marxism versus capitalism is the current excuse, but if it weren't that it would be something else. This capacity for division in the world is quite profound and concerns me greatly because I believe the more coherent the global system is, the better everyone will do. If these divisions are allowed to dominate, we may end up with a much more fragmented situation, one in which the US drifts away from Europe and turns towards the Pacific basin; Europe turns much more to Eastern Europe and the Soviet Union; while South America turns towards Africa and south-east Asia. Such a world seems plausible to me—and not a very happy one.

The fifth force is a possible global transformation towards a new economic order. It requires greater wisdom, much more interconnection, a willingness to experience the process of creative destruction and economic evolution. I don't believe change happens easily or painlessly; it is a difficult process for individuals, companies, countries and the world. The outcome of such a process is likely to lead us to a very diverse world and a much more efficient one in terms of its use of environment, resources and energy. It will be a very dynamic environment but also a very competitive and even difficult one, because nothing comes without a price. Even this world may not necessarily be a happy one in many ways; but it will on the whole, I feel, be a better one.

The key to the future is the willingness to adapt and face the necessity of change. I think one of the fundamentals is to achieve a degree of coherence in the world economy—and multinationals can play a role in this. These companies are reasonably good vehicles for spreading information and getting things done, and in the end they always conform to nature. Nature always wins; it always forces us to change and live within the bounds of our natural environment, for if we don't, we die—just like the dinosaurs. We are not above or below the system; we *are* the system—and we are passing through a time of great stress and some danger. All this leads me to maintain a sense of humility about how much we can know about the future and what the eventual outcome will be. However, it's extremely important to have a realistic view of what is possible and what is not, and to be able to separate the realm of choice from that of necessity, because otherwise choices have no meaning.

I conclude with an observation made by the chairman of the editorial board of Japan's biggest newspaper, when I went to see him two years ago as part of a study I was doing for Shell on the future of that country. I had interviewed a number of people who had identified the huge problems facing Japan: the fact that the population is getting old very fast; that the values of the youth are changing; that the world wants trade protection against it and so on. I asked this man: "Can you be optimistic about Japan's future in the face of all these problems?" He replied, "Oh, I'm very optimistic." When I asked how that was so, he said: "In Japan we have two words for optimism. One is the kind of optimism a young person feels in looking to old age, that it will be a harmonious time without troubles and cares—the sort of utopia you in the West long for. It is the anticipation of a future in which every problem is solved. But there's a second word for optimism in Japan. It means having enough challenges in life to give it meaning. It is in this sense that I'm very optimistic about the future."

From a European to a World Economic Community

Bernard Zamaron

Bernard Zamaron, from Luxembourg, is EEC Consultant to the General Directorate of Credit and Investment. A dedicated believer in the spiritual ideals underlying the European Community, he is founder of the Robert Schuman Centre for Europe.

The European Economic Community is reputed to be a monster—all the more terrifying because, unlike the Loch Ness Monster, it can be seen in the form of its bureaucrats; and I am one of them. We are considered a very bureaucratic organisation, but this is a questionable point, since there are, I think, less people involved in running the whole EEC than in running the Greater London Council.

I am responsible for borrowing and loan matters within the EEC. Our department is 75 people strong, including secretaries, and we have a turnover of £1 billion a year. If you ask a bank whether employing 75 people to make a £1 billion a year turnover in borrowing, loans and investment programmes is excessively bureaucratic, you will find to the contrary that possibly ten times that number would be involved in the bank situation. I am responsible for contact between my department, the European Parliament and the Council of Ministers, but part of my job is to follow up on the loans we have made. For example, we have set up a scheme to finance job creation and I see to it that these investments are carried out and the jobs created. Of course, in the future there must be an emphasis on creating work rather than jobs, but I would say that in the transitional period it is important that we still create jobs. It is a similar situation to giving food aid to countries of the southern hemisphere. Some people say that food aid is perverse. Of course it is perverse; we must build an economy for these countries within which they can feed themselves. Meanwhile, however, we have

138

to feed those people or they will starve. It is the same with the transformation from jobs to work.

We have financed thousands of jobs all over the European Community to give employment to former coal and steel workers whose pits or works have been closed. This is an example of cooperative economy and it stems from the time of the first European Treaty in 1951. This treaty contained a new idea: that the workers concerned—coal and steel workers, that is—should not suffer because of changes in Europe's economy and that those who lose their jobs because of changes in markets or in technical methods of production should be re-employed at the cost of the community. Additionally, the coal and steel community was not based, as is the EEC, on a budget of general taxation within member states. It was a partial community financed by a special levy of 0.3% on coal and steel production. Thus, the total coal and steel enterprise of member states was made responsible for finding other employment for workers when their jobs were lost.

The work of the EEC also helps to promote progress. For instance, the other day I was visiting a very interesting British company which produces optical fibres made of absolutely pure glass—possibly the purest in Europe. Each fibre can carry 15,000 telephone conversations at the same time. This is the kind of development the EEC can help support.

My main interest, however, is in the community aspect of the EEC. Harold Macmillan, the former prime minister of Britain, once said to an audience in Oxford: "You have not understood anything. It is not a common market, it is a community." I was very pleased to hear such a statement from a person in his position. To see the EEC as a common market is completely different from seeing it as a community. A common market is inward looking, materialistically oriented and bent upon defending its own interests. It is motivated by fear, which can lead to aggression. Napoleon I tried to create a common market about 180 years ago. It was not a community; it was an aggressive proposition. In the same way, if we think of the EEC only as a common market, it results in the kind of difficulty surrounding the negotiations on the entry of Spain into the EEC, with the French fruit producers, backed by the Italians, not wanting Spain to join because it might hurt their own economic position. If we think of the EEC as a community, however, the situation is completely different. A community is outward looking and spiritually oriented; it is based on love and is open to the world. Looking at the question of Spain's entry to the EEC from this angle we see that we must allow them in because they are part of our people and our culture.

So it is a question of motivation: on one side there is fear and selfishness, on the other there is openness and love. It is very important to distinguish between these attitudes in any negotiation at EEC level, because the one can lead only to tension, while the other admits the possibility of dialogue.

At the Findhorn Foundation people talk about and practise attunement. Although the ministers of the European Council do not join hands before they begin their sessions, the whole process is nevertheless one of attunement. The members of the European Parliament also try to attune to one another, but they are always able to vote on issues as well, so it is not imperative. They do attempt to achieve attunement, however, and often a compromise amendment comes up where several party groups decide to make a common proposal—usually in connection with world issues such as Nicaragua, South Africa or others.

In the Council of Ministers the principle of attunement is important because decisions can be made more or less only when there is unanimity—or, to put it negatively, only when no country exercises its veto, even if in many cases this veto possibility is not a right but just an agreement to disagree dating from De Gaulle's time. Sometimes it takes the Council a long time to reach decisions but this I will never criticise, because every little detail must be taken into account. The results of those decisions affect the lives of many people throughout Europe and you cannot by a majority vote let down the fishermen of Scotland or milk producers on the Continent. You must try to find the right solution for one and all.

The process of creating the Community is a difficult one, but it is a process for a new world and is not achieved in one day, or even one year or one decade. The reason why we sometimes have a lot of difficulty is that although a night of discussions can create a real atmosphere of attunement among the ministers so that by the morning they give up their selfish positions, the official administrators of the various countries, who are also present, often try in the following few days to regain their national positions somewhat. This can result in near breakdown of the agreement reached in the earlier mood of attunement and is a problem we have not yet overcome.

The concept of the European Community was based on the idea of Robert Schuman that after two world wars we should do away with relationships based on force (which besides being military can also be economic) to create an organisation where the interest of all would be taken into account and where decisions would be taken together. It was he who, as foreign minister of France, launched the idea of the Community on May 9, 1950 by proposing a first step with coal and steel. He made his decision to propose his plan at the perfect moment: if he had left it until the next day, the situation would already have changed and the opportunity would have been missed.

The European Community came about through the attunement of three leaders—Schuman, Adenauer and De Gasperi—who had the same spiritual conviction and had suffered in similar ways through the wars. It is a community born out of silence and long meditation. We have to take into consideration the fact that the European Community arose after a hundred years of wars. It did not happen just by chance but came about because people decided to create it—and then channelled into the construction of a new Europe all the grace generated by people's suffering during the wars—those who died in concentration camps, in bombed cities and on battlefields. If you speak with the survivors, they tell you that the last wish of many of those who died was that there should be a different world afterwards, and it seems to me that a tremendous energy was created all over Europe which has been channelled into making this historic change possible. The change is felt by other continents too. They no longer bother very much about the way EEC countries quarrel amongst themselves. They see a new world beginning.

An ambassador of a West Indies country recently said that the most important thing in the world is what is being created in and from Europe. The European Community is progressively producing a world cooperative economy. A new intercontinental relationship has been established between the ten European countries on the one side and a group of African, Caribbean and Pacific countries on the other. This relationship is known as 'Lomé'—the name of the capital city of Tobago where the convention has already been signed twice for periods of five years. The vital interests and the means of livelihood of all involved are systematically taken into consideration at this round table, and communal decisions are made with mutual respect. Nobody is left alone in their corner. Even if problems cannot be resolved in a minute or a year, plans are made to create answers. Above all, a common responsibility is felt to arrive at a positive solution.

Even if, as far as the achievements of the European Community are concerned, the daily press give much less attention to the Lomé convention than to the mountains of butter, 'Lomé' is nevertheless the manifestation of a fundamental change in international relationships. As for Europe, where countries have fought one another for centuries, there has been a shift from relations based on force—financial, economic and ideological, even if not military—to those based on searching together for what is right for one and all.

Other communities are building themselves on the model of the European one—the Central American Common Market, for example, and the Andean Pact or, in southern Asia, the ASEAN. This creates the possibility for our progressively building a world of communities dialoguing with one another. This is the only chance we have of getting the countries of the world out of their habitual confrontation for power, because community relationships are not related to power, they are related to spirit. The process of dialoguing and negotiation also allows communities to strengthen themselves internally, because each member has to be aware of the situation in every other country in order to formulate a common position for the group.

Of course, the basis of the European Economic Community is economic, but if we see the whole thing as *only* economic it is like seeing the Findhorn Foundation only as a place where people grow vegetables together and eat them together. The most important thing to understand is that the EEC has been born from a spiritual principle. We are responsible for making it work and become what it is meant to be. Personally, the reason I am still a civil servant in the Community and have not taken advantage of several opportunities for the golden handshake is because I feel this work is vital: it is a unique source of peace for the world. People may think that is an exaggerated statement, but consider: the two world wars did not arise from Asia, Africa or America; they started in Europe. That is why it is appropriate to think that the answer also can come from Europe.

Reflections on a Paradigm Shift in Economics

Manfred Max-Neef

Manfred Max-Neef is a Chilean economist who has worked on many projects in Latin America. He is Founder Director of the Centre for Study and Promotion of Urban, Rural and Development Alternatives, and author of **From the Outside Looking In: Experiences in Barefoot Economics**. *In 1983 he was joint winner of the Right Livelihood Award.*

Many people today are realising that certain aspects of conventional economic theory do not work any more, and are consequently involved in the search for alternatives. What is needed is a paradigm shift. Now, whenever a paradigm shift appears to be necessary, it is because the traditional paradigm is no longer capable of providing adequate answers to important problems that we perceive to be arising. We are at present in a process of transition on this planet which implies the need for such a shift. It often happens, however, that during these periods of transition people regard anything different they do as alternative, and it becomes a somewhat frivolous concept. So I wish to be more precise in this respect. A paradigm shift in economics is not doing just *anything* different; rather, it involves finding very concrete answers to precisely those important problems which cannot be solved by the conventional theories.

Dramatic paradigm shifts have occurred in almost all the sciences during this century. Physics and other natural sciences went through a crisis mainly at the beginning of the century, with the result that they have to a large degree now moved away from their former mechanistic and reductionist interpretation of the universe and, even if they have not completely given it up, have at least established what the limits of that vision are. Very few disciplines at this stage still adhere to a mechanistic and reductionist vision of the universe. Strangely enough, however, some still do. Biology seems to be one. Economics is the other.

The past three decades have been called 'International Development Decades'—at least, the first two were. Since they didn't work, the name of the third was changed to 'International Development Strategy Decade'. It still doesn't work but we have learned some important lessons during that time which I want to point out.

First, we have discovered that the population of any Third World country can be divided into two main groups. One group consists of people directly or indirectly involved with some kind of development strategy normally designed by the governmental agencies of the country. The other consists of the people, usually the majority, dedicated to designing their own survival strategy. We have also learned that these two segments don't mix; they co-exist in a dialectic struggle. Furthermore, the second group has increased, not only in absolute numbers but also relatively.

The mechanistic economic theories that consider growth essential for development—and the more growth the more development—haven't worked. The belief that if there is enough growth there is a trickle-down effect as a result of which the poor become less poor has failed. On the contrary, in most of the countries involved, wealth is more polarised than it was thirty years ago, although there are, of course, some exceptions.

In addition, these mechanistic approaches have tended to make one particular development model predominant all over the world. Third World countries were thought above all to need a process of rapid industrialisation. So industrialisation has been the fundamental goal, and we see the consequences of that today in several serious problems such as the hyper-urbanisation that causes the decay of rural areas and small and medium-sized cities; in unemployment and under-employment; and in the growth of the informal sectors, the underground economies and the survival trades and strategies.

We are now facing situations for which we no longer have answers in terms of conventional economics. One such situation is growth with growing unemployment. Most serious economic analysts today probably recognise that not only does unemployment grow during periods of recession but also it decreases only very little during periods of recovery. This means that even when growth is occurring, the trend is towards increasing unemployment. In other words, the well-known correlation between growth and employment no longer holds. Another problem for which we have no solution is the immense growth of the cities. In 1950, only two of the 15 largest cities in the world were in the Third World. Today 12 of them are. In 1970, there were only 16 cities in the Third World with more than four million inhabitants. By the end of this decade there will be 61. One of the largest cities today is Mexico City, which by the beginning of the next decade will have close to 31 million people in one urban area. One of the shanty towns within Mexico City—Ciudad Netzahualcoyotl—has five million inhabitants.

Something has evidently gone very wrong and we need to correct the situation. The cause of these problems, in my view, lies mainly in the mechanistic and reductionist vision of society held by modern economics. We need a new, more holistic approach.

In order to construct a new paradigm, economics could look to other disciplines for a little inspiration, because we may after all end this century by rediscovering that all disciplines are interrelated, as both the Greeks and mediaeval thinkers realised. In physics particularly, which was the inspiration of economics 200 years ago, we find a totally new image of the world. José Lutzenberger has talked of the concept of Gaia, so I don't need to repeat it. What I wish to add to this is the new vision of quantum physics in relation to the universe. The most interesting hypothesis at the moment—one developed mainly by David Bohm in Britain—is that the whole universe is probably a sort of holo- gram. Holography is an extremely interesting concept. A hologram is analogous to a photograph, but is taken without a lens. Laser light waves are registered in a plaque as a distribution pattern of points and waves. When I look at the plaque, I don't see anything I can decipher, but if I pass another laser beam through it, the original object emerges from the plaque in three dimensions in the air. What is most interest- ing, however, is that if I enlarge just a portion, say a face, from an ordinary photograph, I will end up with a bigger face; but if I pass a laser beam through a similar part of a hologram, what I get is the whole person again, not just a part of them. This is an extraordinary charac- teristic of holography. It means that each part of the whole contains the total information about the object, so that it can be completely reconstructed starting from any one of its components. The total is contained in each part. David Bohm has applied this concept to the universe itself. It is important to stress this aspect of what is happening in physics, because here we see convergences with other streams that come from mysticism or transcendence. There are also older philoso- phical concepts, such as that of Leibnitz, who saw the universe in terms of monads, each of which somehow contained information about the total universe. We can probably say that Leibnitz was the first to conceive the idea of holography.

The holographic hypothesis is an extremely important one which can give us greater insight into the functioning not only of the universe but also of society; and in developing a new economics we must, in my opinion, take these ideas into consideration. We live in a world dominated by a oneness, in which each individual part contains information about the whole and is therefore significant both as a unit and as part of the totality. This idea is confirmed by the Gaia hypothesis, which shows that we humans are part of a larger system that is alive in itself.

What then should be our paradigm for an alternative developmental economics? As I mentioned earlier, the foundations of conventional economics are mechanistic. If we need a new paradigm, we must know where to start from. I propose the following as a starting postulate for such a new paradigm: simply this, that development has to do with people and not with objects.

If development has to do with people, what criteria can I use to judge whether one development process is better than another? Using conventional economic theory, I used to say, "Well, this one is better because the Gross National Product is growing faster." I can't say that any more; I must complement it with something else. Starting from my new postulate, I would say that the better development process is one which causes a greater improvement in the quality of people's lives. But what do I mean by 'quality of life'? It is one of many terms in vogue which people use a lot but don't generally know what they mean by it. I see it as the possibility available—or not available—to people to satisfy their fundamental human needs. However, this still leaves us in the dark because we also have to define human needs, and this is a particularly difficult task since there is a predominant belief that needs are changing all the time. There is an assumption that needs are different in each culture, that they change through history and that they tend to be infinite. Now, if that were true, it would be methodologically impossible to work with the question of human needs. However, a group of us who are attempting to design a human-scale economics have come to the conclusion that this belief is not in fact true, because what is normally not taken into consideration or made explicit is the fundamental difference between a need itself and the method of satisfying that need; that is, the difference between needs and satisfiers. Hence, we have defined a system of nine fundamental human needs, which all interrelate in a permanent interplay. These fundamental needs are in our opinion the same for every human being in every culture and in any period of history. They are the needs for permanance or subsistence; for protection; for affection or love; for understanding; for participation; the need for leisure; for creation; for identity; and for freedom.

It is very difficult for me to conceive that there may be human beings who do not have these needs or that these needs are not or have not been present in different cultures and periods of history. What varies from culture to culture or through time is not the needs themselves but the way in which they are satisfied or not.

Therefore we can say first, that fundamental human needs are few and classifiable; second, that they are the same everywhere; and third, that what essentially defines a culture is not the needs of its people but the satisfiers through which that culture meets these needs or not. In a consumer society there will probably be a high level of satisfaction of certain needs, such as that for subsistence, and a very low level of satisfaction of some of the others. In essence there are two fundamental categories of human needs—those of having and those of being. Traditionally, developmental economics has been exclusively concerned with the needs of having, and it has been assumed that only after those needs are satisfied can we think of satisfying the needs of being—again a mechanistic approach. However, the needs of both having and being not only can but must be met simultaneously. For instance, a capitalistic, hierarchical, authoritarian form of production may satisfy our needs of having, but it is also possible to have an equally efficient production system which is cooperative and in which there are more possibilities for creation and participation. Both sets of needs *can* be met through the economic process. Whether we can allow for a more adequate satisfaction of the entire system of human needs depends on how we organise our economic systems.

Two of the nine fundamental human needs—freedom and participation—have a particular characteristic, a dual characteristic in fact. Freedom is not only a human need but a condition under which people must live in order to be able to satisfy the entire system. If freedom does not exist, access to the satisfaction of many of the other needs will be blocked. And participation is not only a human need, it is also a process, a way of doing things. This means that in creating a new economic paradigm we must understand what makes human participation possible. The possibilities of human participation are determined by a natural law of size. It is absolutely impossible to have participation in a gigantic system; it can only occur at the human scale—in other words, where people have a face and a name, where they mean something to each other and are not simply statistical abstractions. A participatory group is one that has a mathematical structure of such a type that each of the elements is in communication with all of the others and can receive information from them. Mathematically this is called a compact graph; socially, we call it an egalitarian or participatory structure.

If the number of elements grows, however, something complicated happens. Five elements form ten links. If we add one, it will go up to 15 links; and if we add a seventh, it will go up to 21 links. The linkages grow exponentially. In other words, when the number of people grows, the linkages grow so much faster that there comes a point at which the only possibility is to establish a hierarchical structure, because only that can support a large group. If you go beyond the critical size, you inevitably become authoritarian. It is impossible to avoid it. This is a very important point to keep in mind. You cannot have a participatory mass; it is naturally impossible. You have to subdivide it into human-scale groups.

The critical size of a participatory group will of course be determined by the function of that group. If it is a guerrilla band, it must be very small because it has to make very fast decisions. Guerrilla groups anywhere practically never consist of more than 32 people. There may be a lot of groups but the units themselves are never larger than that because any individual member of the group must be able to make decisions and communicate them to the others as quickly as possible. An army division, on the other hand, can consist of 10,000 people because an army has a hierarchical structure which can organise those people. If the purpose of a group is something like looking after a city, it can be larger than a guerrilla band and still participatory because the time it requires to make its decisions can be longer. So size of group is also related to time. But in any case, a participatory group will never be very large.

It is interesting that since the time of the Greeks this principle of size has totally disappeared from human thought. For Aristotle and Plato it was a very concrete and specific concern. Aristotle said that among other things, in order to achieve the *summmum bonum*—the really good life—which is a very ample concept in Aristotelian politics, a city state should never be bigger than what a person could take in at one glance.

Plato was even more specific. He stated that a city should never grow beyond the point where it risked losing its identity and unity. He even went so far as to say that no city should have more than exactly 5,040 families, which may sound funny but is quite extraordinary if we relate it to what we have been saying about critical size. He arrived at the number 5,040 because it is the smallest number simultaneously divisible by 1, 2, 3, 4, 5, 6, 7, 8, 9, 10 and 12. "So what?" you might say. In my opinion he was very clearly perceiving the connection between the critical size of a group, its purpose and the time required for communication in relation to its purpose. He saw that for tax purposes, for example, the total population could be divided into groups of the appropriate size, while in the case of war it could be divided by another number into units of a different size. In other words, this formed the basis for an enormously versatile society; it could be divided into 2, 4, 5, 7, or 12 or however many parts depending on the communication requirements of each group *vis-a-vis* a given challenge.

Well, we don't need to be quite so precise; it would be absurd and we might all become maniacs. The important thing is the message: we cannot be participatory in gigantic units. What happens in trying to reach a consensus is that the bigger the group the more irrelevant the consensus, because you can only agree on trivial things. Triviality also grows exponentially in relation to the size of the group, so you end up agreeing on the most irrelevant points. In a small group you have to think hard, you have to convince the other individuals, so when you reach consensus it's on a deeper level; it will never be trivial.

Within any country we can and should distinguish between three levels—local, regional and national. What traditionally happens in the application of conventional economic models is that development plans are devised at the national level and then imposed on the other levels. But each level has a different metabolism and social rhythm. Time passes in a different way in a small village than in the city of London, because time has nothing to do with a clock; it is something we *feel*, a sense of duration. Five minutes of toothache are much longer than five minutes with a person we love. The sensation of duration is different. This is the kind of difference between the three levels, so there is a problem of social rhythms when one level is imposed on the others. From a strategic point of view this means that whatever can potentially be solved at the local level *must* be solved there. The same holds for the regional and national levels. You should not do locally what definitely cannot be done at that level. It would be ridiculous to have a local telephone system; you obviously need a national telecommunications system. But there are many things that can be dealt with at a local level, thereby increasing local self-reliance, which leads in turn to self-reliance at the regional level and, as an aggregation of that, more self-reliance at the national level. This is precisely what we need in relation to the economic crisis today.

So, to go back to the nine fundamental human needs, this system can help us orient our development strategies and projects in such a way that they allow the people who are involved and affected to satisfy these needs to the greatest extent possible. This system of needs is also useful for reinterpreting the concept of poverty. Poverty is one of the reductionist concepts of economics and is defined in terms of income thresholds: anyone below a certain income is poor, and anyone below another certain income is extremely poor. But in human-scale economics we talk not about poverty but about *poverties*, in the sense that any fundamental human need that is not adequately satisfied is a human poverty. So we can talk about poverty of understanding, poverty of identity and, in many places today, poverty of freedom and so forth.

If we use this view as a reference point, suddenly all concepts of First World, Second World and Third World—which have also been established in terms of conventional economic indicators—begin to vanish, and we are just left with human beings everywhere. Then it makes sense for a Scottish farmer to talk to a Brazilian farmer. They have much more in common than we think, if we understand them as human beings with these fundamental needs and not in terms of a GNP. Why should a GNP determine whether we can dialogue or not? It generates tremendous inferiority complexes. We in Chile are said to be underdeveloped. It's outrageous! Why should we accept that we are underdeveloped because our *per capita* GNP is less than that of Luxembourg? In fact, if we look closely, we may see that the so-called underdeveloped countries are far more advanced than the 'developed' countries in the satisfaction of certain fundamental human needs. In many of these countries the needs of being are probably more important and better satisfied than in the rich countries, which concentrate mainly on satisfying the needs of having. In fact, it is possible to see a constant needs trade-off happening, so that when a certain need is clearly under-satisfied, the system tries to compensate by satisfying some of the other needs at a higher level. For instance, in poverty-stricken areas you often find forms of solidarity and mutual aid that satisfy at a very high level the needs for protection, affection and participation. In a highly competitive system it is precisely those needs that are undersatisfied, and you find the classic example of the chap who is very rich but very unhappy and who ends up committing suicide because nobody loves him.

In employing this vision of a holistic economics we can complement the traditional indicators of wealth, which not only are dangerous and generate complexes, but which also do not even indicate what they are supposed to. The GNP, for example, has two very strange characteristics. First, it is based on an arithmetic that would be unacceptable on page one of the simplest arithmetic book in elementary school: the only sign that exists is plus; you can only add, never subtract. So any process that generates a monetary flux or a market transaction is acceptable. It is totally irrelevant whether it is productive, unproductive or destructive—it all adds to the GNP. In other words, if I want my GNP to grow in order to impress the International Monetary Fund, I can, for instance, quickly and 'efficiently' depredate a fundamental natural resource and I will have a beautiful GNP. If I am lucky enough to have a tremendous epidemic in my country, with my whole population getting sick and consuming a large amount of drugs, my GNP will also grow. The fuller the hospitals are, the better. There are many ways in which I can make that magic thing, the GNP, grow.

Secondly, since the GNP takes into account only what happens in the market, any activities that do not generate a monetary transaction are not represented—in other words, traditional economics supposes that such activities do not generate wealth. This includes everything done at home to care for and educate children, all the housework, buying, travelling and household maintenance activities and everything done at subsistence levels. All this is done mostly by women, and by groups that live at subsistence levels. More than half of humanity is simply invisible to conventional economics, and what they do seems to have no economic significance. It is quite fantastic that the husband of a woman who works for maybe 12 or 14 hours each day in her house can say, "My wife doesn't work." And consider the situation of two neighbours, who each have five children and work hard all day at home. They have no economic value whatever, but suppose one day Mary says to Jane, "Look, why don't we do this: from tomorrow I will do all the things in your house, and you will do all the things in my house, and at the end of the month I'll pay you £500 and you'll pay me £500." If they do that, the GNP grows. Furthermore, if a man marries his housekeeper, the GNP goes down because she becomes a wife who has no value, whereas as a housekeeper she does. This is the kind of indicator we have to do away with, or at least improve.

The great Spanish philosopher Ortega y Gasset used to say that every period in history has its particular theme or preoccupation, which is the determinant for the behaviour of that period. Efficiency, it seems, is the preoccupation of the present age, but it is clear that this has not always been the theme. If it had been, nobody would have built those marvellous cathedrals in the 12th and 13th centuries. They obviously didn't come about through a system of bids on the free market, with whoever made the best bid building Cologne cathedral, for example. The theme during that period was transcendence, a theme which allowed for all the things that happened during the mediaeval period. But we are obsessed by efficiency, so we are able to justify things like the depredation of the Amazon. What needs to be included in the new economics is a different concept of efficiency, one that goes beyond monetary indicators to take into account aspects like sustainability of process and resources and the satisfaction of human needs. The more a system allows for the satisfaction of these needs, the more efficient it will be; and the more sustainable a process is in terms of human and natural resources, the more efficient it will be—even in monetary terms. We have to combine all these aspects in order to have a more holistic and humanistic concept of efficiency.

Finally, another fundamental necessity for a new economics is, in my opinion, the recovery of something we have lost during this century— particularly during these last three decades—and that is variety and diversity. For a long time we have preferred uniformity and monotony, because they are believed to be more efficient. One of my visions of the end of the world is not a holocaust but a point at which everything becomes so uniform and monotonous that in order to know where we are we have to read a signpost. This would be followed by a time when we reach maximum entropy and die because of total loss of energy. You can see the tendency to uniformity even in political and social organisations. Uniformity brings uniforms—and the world is full of them. Everywhere more and more authoritarian structures and systems are emerging, particularly in Third World countries. There *are* groups who are conscious that diversity should be preserved, but I am honestly worried that diversity is decreasing—at least from the point of view of the Latin American countries, which are being dramatically influenced by the richer countries through television, which the people absorb subliminally.

This trend towards uniformity can be seen not only in society but also—perhaps more importantly—in agriculture. Fifty thousand hectares of wheat seem to be more efficient than a polyculture of different products, which has more sustainability and is less vulnerable. This concept has led us into extreme danger, the genetic erosion of plant resources. Few people seem worried about this. They are much more concerned with the possibility of a nuclear holocaust, but that after all depends on whether some fool presses the button; as long as it isn't pressed, the holocaust does not happen. The genetic erosion of plant resources, however, is an ongoing process that is rapidly depriving the world of its genetic variety. India, for example, grew 30,000 varieties of rice at the beginning of this century, but now there are only 15 left. Of all the varieties of onions that existed in Egypt only one remains and that is a so-called 'improved' kind. Improved varieties have to be reinforced with germ-plasm from the original varieties, but those are disappearing so rapidly that soon there will be no possibility of sustaining these processes and there will be complete genetic breakdown. This implies that within the next 10 or 15 years, if there is not some dramatic turn-around, we are distinctly and irreversibly *through*, with or without a nuclear holocaust.

I hope what I have said goes beyond a simple criticism of our existing economic system to share some thinking about what a new economics should contain.

Gaian Economics

José Lutzenberger

José Lutzenberger, a self-employed agronomist and consultant in organic agriculture and soft technologies, is Brazil's premier advocate of environmental awareness. He is Founder Director of AGAPAN, the first citizens' environmental group in Brazil.

The concept of Gaia was first presented in the book *Gaia* by James Lovelock, a British climatologist, and also by an American, Lynn Margulis, one of the great biologists of our time. Less emotional ecologists use the term 'ecosphere' to designate the great functional unit which is the biosphere, atmosphere, lithosphere and hydrosphere acting together in concert. Lovelock chose 'Gaia', an emotion-laden word, on purpose and he deliberately chose a feminine name because he sees the ecosphere not just as a dead, functional, cybernetically balanced unit, but as a living being in its own right, and this is really what Gaia is. Life on this planet is one super-organism and we humans and millions of other species are only cells in its tissues.

In his book Lovelock gives us many instances of the finely-tuned cybernetic mechanisms of recycling and climate control that have both made life possible on this planet and enabled it to survive for three and a half billion years, evolving and diversifying into an incredible symphony of organic evolution, of which we are only a very small—although lately a very dangerous—part. He explains the operation of the mechanism for recycling the elements vital to life. Life needs about 25 of the approximately 90 elements listed in the table of Mendeleev, and these elements—carbon, oxygen, hydrogen, nitrogen, sulphur, potassium, calcium, sodium, magnesium, manganese, iron, copper, cobalt and so on—must be constantly recycled. If this had not happened, life would have come to an end billions of years ago. Sulphur, for example, a very important element in living beings, would soon be depleted on the continents if it were not recycled, and it was only recently discovered to be recycled by very special types of algae that live in the fertile waters of the continental shelves. Each of the elements is constantly recycled from land to ocean to atmosphere and back to land. If we were wise, we would take care not to demolish Gaia, not to destroy or interfere with those cycles. But unfortunately modern industrial society has unleashed processes and forms of human behaviour that do exactly that.

There is a small but very fast-growing group of people who are concerned about these problems and who want to stop this demolition of Gaia. To do this we must understand where we are going wrong. In its present form modern industrial society rests on a series of false assumptions—tenets and postulates that are contrary to the laws of life and nature. Its working hypothesis doesn't account for the existence of Gaia or for its cybernetic balancing mechanisms. It doesn't account for the fact that we *depend* on Gaia, that Gaia can survive without us but we cannot survive without Gaia. Actually Gaia was there billions of years before we appeared as a species on this planet. What is three or four million years compared to three and a half *billion* years since life first structured itself on this planet in the so-called primaeval consommé? At that time the first organic molecules of a certain complexity were formed; then for maybe a billion years organic chemical evolution took over, followed by cellular evolution. More and more complex organisms evolved until, about 600 billion years ago at the end of the geological period called the Pre-Cambrian, we had relatively complex creatures in the ocean. One hundred or two hundred million years later, the first organisms crept out of the ocean and colonised the land. Gaia is much older than we are and Gaia *can* survive without us—but we cannot survive without Gaia.

If we are smart, we may become, as it were, the grey tissue of Gaia's brain. We can take over as conductors of the great symphony. But if we are foolish, we may be cast off like the bacteria in the pus of an infected wound. Gaia will continue. She will fall back to some earlier—maybe simpler—forms, but there are another five billion years to go before our sun becomes too hot and swallows the Earth and then slowly dies down into a red dwarf.

Lovelock explains a very interesting aspect of how Gaia controls the conditions for her own survival. What we know as life on Earth is possible only within an extremely narrow range of temperatures—between 0°C and about 50°C. A few very rare forms of bacteria can

155

survive in hot water up to 70°C but most living beings would die at above 50°C. However, our sun today is twice as hot as it was when life first appeared on this planet, while mean temperatures have stayed relatively stable. How Gaia has achieved that stability of temperature is by extracting carbon dioxide (CO_2) from the atmosphere and storing it in the ground in the form of fossil deposits such as carbonates, coal, lignite, peat, natural gas and in the biomass of living systems, especially in the great tropical rainforests and in soil humus. But we humans today—we who consider ourselves so intelligent and superior to nature—are putting all that carbon dioxide back into the atmosphere by destroying our forests, by degrading the humus in our soils and by burning our fossil deposits, which in our greed we call fossil *fuels*, as if they had been created only for us. Small wonder that it already looks as if the climate is becoming unhinged, especially in the past few years. We have had climatic irregularities all over the world. Where it should have been raining, it has been dry and *vice versa*. In my home state in Brazil, for example, we had about five months of almost continuous rain when we should have had dry weather, while another state right next to us had almost five months of continuous drought. In Europe it has been hot when it should have been cold, and cold when it should have been hot. These may be only momentary fluctuations that occur every 50 or 100 years or so, but on the other hand they may augur something much more serious to come.

Modern industrial society is fumbling with all of Gaia's finely tuned mechanisms of control. Not only are we messing with the carbon dioxide equilibrium, we are also, among other things, upsetting the ozone balance, putting more dust into the atmosphere, increasing the cloud cover with aerosols and changing the reflectivity of the soil when we destroy forests. When rain falls in areas of rainforest, within about 40 hours 70% of the water is back in the atmosphere because of the fantastic evapo-transpiration rate in such areas. When you cut the forest down and leave naked soil in its place, the almost vertical rays of tropical sun heat the soil up to 50-60°C and instead of evapo-transpiration taking place, which forms new clouds and allows rain to recycle (as happens in South America, for example, five or six times between the Atlantic and the eastern flanks of the Andes), you get hot updraughts that dissolve the clouds.

We are acting as if we were a bunch of little apes in the cockpit of a big plane, playing around with the control mechanisms without knowing what we are doing—and the plane is already shaking. Why are we acting that way? Why are we now at the point where the scale of our interference in Gaia's metabolism is comparable to the scale of that metabolism itself? Why are we fumbling with all these finely tuned mechanisms of homeostasis?

Modern industrialism could be compared to a fanatical religious movement. It is much more fanatical and ferocious than was, for example, the advance of Islam in the Mediterranean basin a millennium ago. It is a movement with a missionary zeal, with rewards for its priests and with a force of conviction unparallelled by any of the old traditional religions. This is why it is so successful. It has already conquered almost the whole planet. The very few remaining original and unique cultures that still cling to the old ways are even now being destroyed or absorbed. As soon as such people encounter this fanatical religion, not only do they adhere to it but they also feel demoralised. Anyone who has seen South American Indians coming into contact with what we call civilisation knows what I am talking about. They immediately become *totally* demoralised and absolutely helpless. There has never before been such a religion, capable of doing what this one is doing to all other cultures. There is actually only one culture left on this planet—industrial culture. All the others seem doomed to disappear. I hope we can still perhaps save a few, but it means we must all become aware of what is happening.

Our missionary zeal is such that we *want* other cultures to change. A few months ago I was talking to an official of our Indian Agency, arguing in favour of the preservation of the few remaining Indian cultures. He was shocked. He said, "But these people live sub-human lives. We must help them become civilised. We must integrate them into our consumer society. They don't even know money yet—imagine! How backward they are!"

Today we divide the world into developed and underdeveloped countries and the stated aim of all governments is to develop the last underdeveloped country. We want everybody to become like people in New York. This is what foreign aid is for—to help those backward people become 'modernised'. The Amazon forest, which is still intact in its glorious primaeval form, is considered the most backward place in the world—no elevators, no planes, no big buildings, just intact forest. "It simply cannot remain that way," we say. "We must do something to develop it!"

Peter Schwartz from Shell mentioned a $5 billion aluminium factory project that they are financing in Brazil. This is a tremendously

157

pernicious project. It means demolishing whole mountains and has already marginalised whole Indian tribes whose culture is tens of thousands of years old and from whom we can learn very much. They have simply been eliminated. Some of them were mown down by machine gun—not by Shell, of course, but by the people who prepared the way for them. The aluminium factory will get its electricity from a big dam which is flooding 200,000 ha of intact primaeval forest. The forest was to have been cut down first and $400 million was even obtained from the World Bank to do so but in the end the money was not used for this purpose and the forest was left standing.

One of the tools used to drive out the inhabitants from that region was a herbicide called 2, 4, 5-T from Dow Chemicals. This product was used in combination with another one, 2, 4-D, in the Vietnam war when tens of thousands of square kilometres of forest were killed by what technocrats and the military euphemistically call 'defoliants' but which in fact are herbicides that completely destroy the forest. In order to move the people from the basin now being flooded without having to compensate them for loss of their land, the developers went into the areas where the big Brazil nut trees and rubber trees grew—which the people depend on for their survival—and painted all those trees with 2, 4, 5-T to kill them so the people would lose their livelihood and have to move away. The same thing is also happening elsewhere. In the state of Acre in the westernmost part of the Brazilian Amazon, big landowners and industrialists from the south are destroying the natural rubber trees by applying herbicides, this time from planes, the way the Americans did in Indo-China, in order to make the people leave. And do you know what they want to do there? They want to *plant* rubber trees—but in big monocultures where they will need to use herbicides, insecticides and fungicides, and from which the profits will enrich a few people who already have too much money. All those people who were making a good living from the natural rubber trees in the forest and who had an interest in the preservation of the forest have been marginalised. They will either become day labourers or will end up starving in some slum.

The beneficiaries of all these enormous projects are a few corrupt Brazilian politicians, some powerful businessmen and some of the big multinationals, be they American, German, French, Dutch or whatever. The Amazon forest is not being destroyed by its own people. It is being destroyed by forces from outside, by people who go there to multiply their capital and who don't even need that money. They move in there, considering it to be an empty place. But it's not empty; it's full of people—people who have a different lifestyle, a very happy and beautiful one, in harmony with nature.

When you talk to the technocrats responsible for these schemes, they always tell you, "Well, we will take care to do what we can to minimise the damage." We humans have a right, of course, to learn by making errors, but there is one type of error we have no right to commit: those with irreversible consequences. Once we have cut down the tropical rainforest, it will not come back. Beneath the rainforests are the poorest soils in the world with absolutely no nutrients, since the nutrients are all in circulation in the forest biomass.

This kind of pernicious behaviour is not typical only of capitalism. It also happens in countries that call themselves communist. Actually, the way I see the difference between communism and capitalism is of the same order as the difference between Catholicism and Protestantism. Catholicism and Protestantism are both Christian; communism and capitalism are both technocratic, both industrialist. In the old traditional religions the priesthood exerted and maintained its power through doctrine and dogma, liturgy and ritual. The priesthood of modern technocracy maintains and builds up its power through a very particular form of ideology and technological infrastructures. One special aspect is that, contrary to traditional religions, this ideology is never openly stated. If you want to know the dogmas of the Catholic Church, you just have to read the catechism and the books of the saints. If you want to know the ideology of communism, all you have to do is read books by Marx, Engels or Lenin and you know exactly what they mean. If you want to know what Hitler planned, you can read about it in his book *Mein Kampf*. But the ideology of modern industrial society, of technocracy, is never openly stated. It is implicit, however, in everything that politicians, public administrators and especially managers say. They want you to take it for common sense—and most of us do. We accept their ideology because it is never openly stated. Even the churches until very recently joined the chorus and went out into the world trying to convert people to 'progress'.

Modern industrial society has many implicit dogmas. I will mention only a few of them here. The first dogma was not invented by technocrats: it comes from the Judaeo-Christian tradition and it is our anthropocentric view of the world. We see ourselves as the only important creatures on this planet. A very few among us—people like Albert Schweitzer and St Francis of Assisi—had a different way of looking at

159

it, but generally in Western culture all non-human creatures, whether they be animals, plants, bacteria, fungi or viruses, are completely outside our system of ethics. There is a famous statement by a Buddhist philosopher who, when he encountered Western thought, exclaimed, "But I will never understand a culture where making love is considered a sin and destroying a tree 500 years old is not."

For us, cutting down a whole forest is *not* a sin. Brazilian technocrats are cutting down hundreds of thousands of kilometres of forest and are destroying one of the most complicated, fantastic and unknown ecosystems in the world. A European forest has maybe two or three dozen different species of trees; the Amazon forest has more than 2,500 tree species *known* to botanists, and they suspect there are at least 10,000 more that have not been catalogued. For the rich people and technocrats who go to the Amazon to raise cattle, that forest has absolutely no value. It is just something in their way that has to be destroyed. This is perhaps the original sin, the most pernicious of them all, that we have no respect for other creatures and think we are the only important ones in this incredible world. We don't see the world as a fantastic symphony; we see only ourselves. The rest is a kind of resource, something we use if we can and throw away if we cannot take advantage of it.

Another dogma never openly stated is one that is ecologically impossible. As I mentioned previously, Lovelock in his book explains the cycles that keep Gaia alive. All the resources that living systems use are permanently and eternally recycled, with the exception of energy. The living systems of nature work according to a closed circle model. For instance, plants produce oxygen and animals consume it, while animals produce carbon dioxide and plants consume it. So a tree is as much an organ of my organism as are my liver, kidneys and lungs. It is an external organ of mine and I am an external organ of it; we are one system. Modern technocracy doesn't think like that, however. It deals in a completely different model: an infinite and a unidirectional flow into another infinite. It postulates infinite resources on one side and an infinite dump on the other. Of course, the technocrats know that resources eventually are used up but they say, "Well once we use up petroleum, we will develop nuclear fission energy and then nuclear fusion energy. And when we have used up all our iron, copper, aluminium, selenium and so on, we can always find substitutes." So in effect they believe in infinite resources. And when you do something like putting lead in gasoline or mercury in paints or copper and mercury in pesticides, then you believe in an infinite dump too. These very precious materials are being used in such a way that they become uniformly and atomically spread over the planet, with the result that they can never be recovered. This model is lunacy. It doesn't work.

In the closed model system of nature there is no waste. The residues of one are the resources of another. When Indians defecate in the forest, they are fertilising the trees. But when we of industrialised society put dirt into the ground or a river, we are creating pollution, because we are putting it in the wrong place. Sanitary engineers see something fundamentally undesirable in garbage and industrial effluent, so they do things like build enormous dumps to bury it in, and then put trees over it. But it hasn't disappeared; it's just like sweeping dirt under the carpet. There is no undesirable substance on this planet. We should always ask ourselves, "What can we do with it?" and as soon as we do that we will go to the source of the matter. A tannery, for instance, produces a terrible effluent—a stinking, gluey, ugly mess, which contains about 13% solid organic matter and a heavy metal, chrome. Sanitary engineers usually build a big treatment plant where they decant and bury the mud from the tannery, while adding some substances to the water to clean and oxygenise it before returning it to the river as clear water. But the substances they extracted are now in the dump and are very dangerous for future generations who will come across this organic matter contaminated with a heavy metal. If a different philosophy were to be applied, the sanitary engineers would take the chrome from the chrome bath and recycle it; they would extract the organic matter when it appears in the first bath, when the raw leather is treated with calcium and sulphide. Each residue would be treated separately and would be useful. We are actually doing that now in some tanneries in Brazil. It took us some time to convince the farmers that the organic residue was very good fertiliser, so we had to give it to them free at first. Now they fight to buy it and the tannery is making more money.

The philosophy of infinite resources on one side and an infinite dump on the other must be reversed. The only flux that is open is the flux of energy. In the closed circle model, living systems are maintained by an open flux of sunlight. It will eventually come to an end in another five billion years or so, but while it lasts this recycling is, as it were, eternal. Unfortunately, however, we seem to believe in the other model. How else could we do the things we do? We have even set up an agricultural system by which we can only produce today at the expense of the future. We use, for example, phosphorus that comes from mines in North Africa, the Soviet Union, Florida and the north of Brazil, and we allow all the natural nutrients of the soil to wash into the ocean through our sewers.

A third dogma of modern industrial society and one of its most important tenets is its belief in the eternal growth of the economy. If we want our economy to grow 5% in a year and it only grows by 4%, it is considered a crisis. In some instances, of course, growth may be quite desirable. If a child of three ceases to grow, that could be a problem. But if I at the age of 57 were to *continue* to grow, that would also be a calamity. Economists seem to believe that we need an eternally growing economy. This means, in the language of cybernetics, that we are introducing into the system an element of positive feedback. In nature we have several types of behaviour. There are things that don't move; the stone the astronauts found on the surface of the moon, for instance, had not budged for four billion years or more. That is a static situation. Among the dynamic situations in nature we have two extremes. One is what mathematicians call exponential behaviour and the other is what ecologists call homeostatic behaviour. Exponential behaviour is the type you see in a snowball. The snowball receives positive feedback: as it rolls, it becomes bigger because more snow sticks to it, and as it grows, it rolls faster and so on. But this kind of behaviour is inherently unsustainable. It is impossible to keep the snowball rolling eternally: there is not enough slope or snow for it in the whole world. Anyway, long before it can become too big it disintegrates and forms a tremendous avalanche.

This is exactly what is happening today, as long as we keep introducing positive feedback into our economies. We are already reaching the point of avalanche. But apparently economists still think they can help the situation by finding more resources. More resources, however, will mean greater disaster. We may gain a few years but the disaster will be much worse for it. We need to give up the behaviour of the snowball. The snowball can only remain a snowball if we make it stop and place it on a level surface.

We must go for another type of behaviour—not exponential but homeostatic behaviour. When you tell conventional economists—and fortunately there are many who are not conventional any more—that we need a stable situation, they immediately protest, "Oh no, we cannot accept stagnation." But a homeostatic situation can be *tremendously* dynamic. Our sun is a homeostatic situation. It has been shining at about that force for the last four and a half billion years because the outward-pushing forces are perfectly balanced by the inward-pushing ones. We have a homeostatic situation in a tank of water with inlet and outlet. These tanks have a device at their entrance that opens the entrance faucet when too much water goes out and closes it again when too much water comes in. This is negative feedback. Where there is negative feedback there can be an extremely dynamic situation. A tremendous amount of water can flow through that tank but it is a *stable* situation: the water level oscillates within a very narrow range.

Similarly, we could well have a very dynamic economy that is also stable and non-growing. As long as we believe in eternal growth, however, we believe that a snowball has a future when in fact it does not. The longer we keep up the belief in the eternal growth of our economy, the greater is the disaster we prepare for our children.

There are many other fallacies but I think I have mentioned the most important ones. What we need today, if we want a future for our children, is a change to a completely different ideology. Fortunately people *are* beginning to change. Many people have, for instance, given up the idea that money has value in itself. After all, money is more or less an abstraction. Alan Watts, the Buddhist philosopher, once said that modern industrial society is not materialistic, although we sometimes think of ourselves as being so. If we were materialistic, we wouldn't treat matter the way we do. We wouldn't be destroying marvellous things like the Amazon forest; we wouldn't be as wasteful of precious materials. We are not materialists, we are abstractionists. We see only figures in our books. If we were real materialists, we would see real limits. But as long as we concentrate only on figures in books, there are no limits: once we write ten trillion, we can write eight quintillion or whatever. We are destroying the planet because we believe in figures, and once we realise that, we will see that money is interesting only within certain limits. There is a tremendous difference between having £10 in my pocket and having £500 and there's a great difference between £500 and £5 million. But once I have £10 million, what use are £20 million to me? Fortunately, more and more people are beginning to see that, and as we realise it, we will contribute to change.

There are many things we have to do. We must give up our present agricultural methods and learn to farm by using only locally obtainable inputs. That means we must go organic in agriculture. It is perfectly possible to maintain the high yield we have today without using poisons. We have to undertake more reafforestation—but not by planting monocultures of exotic trees the way we do today. We must allow real, complicated, natural forests to grow back—highly balanced cybernetic systems like the tropical forests or the native forests that existed in Europe. We must protect at least a viable part of every form of ecosystem. When we demolish whole mountains, as we are doing in the Carajás project, we destroy whole communities of plants. On those mountains we have some of the most marvellous forms of plant community, and they are all endemic—species that occur in one particular place and nowhere else on the planet. When we wipe out their habitat, the species is gone. When a species disappears, the universe becomes poorer. That species will never come back. Living species hold the accumulated wisdom of hundreds of millions of years of natural evolution and we destroy them as if they mean absolutely nothing. We don't even know what function they perform in Gaia. They may have a very important function, like those algae that are responsible for the recycling of sulphur. We will probably find out when it is too late.

We must also learn to control our population. We cannot continue to behave like bacteria, which always go on a spree when they find a substrate that is good for them; their population starts multiplying rapidly but at a certain point they suddenly all die in their own residues and their population drops to almost zero again. This is our situation today.

Change is an educative process; it cannot happen overnight. One of the most important things is to understand our own technology. Every aspect of our life today is infiltrated by some kind of sophisticated technology. We cannot give it up, at least not immediately, and I don't think we *should* give all of it up. It is interesting that only a very small proportion of people could tell you how, for instance, a television operates—not in technical detail but in principle. How many people could tell you the difference between an ordinary auto engine and a diesel engine? Most people don't know much about these things. And if you ask about something more complicated, such as the technological infrastructures that keep the economy going, then most people know absolutely nothing. What an interesting contradiction! We are a highly—perhaps purely—technological culture but we are all technological illiterates. We are also specialists, which is a fatal situation and all the more dangerous because we don't realise it. Technology in the Middle Ages was quite sophisticated but it was also transparent to everybody—you did not have to be a miller to understand the windmill or the water-wheel. Today most of us can no longer distinguish between technology conceived in the human interest and that conceived in the interests of the powerful.

For example, in my home state in the south of Brazil we have large plantations of peaches and apples and half a dozen very large canning factories. About ten years ago hundreds of women were employed to clean the fruit with knives. Today the fruit is peeled chemically by means of a caustic soda bath. The manager who decided to introduce this new technology acted according to conventional ideology. He introduced an increase in efficiency: now two or three people with a machine can do what it took hundreds of women to do by hand. He was probably convinced that his decision was a merely technical one—nothing to do with ethics or politics. This is another of the implicit dogmas of technocracy, by the way, that technology and science are more or less synonymous and have nothing to do with ethics or politics.

When this manager decided to introduce chemical peeling, he actually caused very serious damage to society in that area. Firstly, hundreds of poor women, who really needed those jobs, even though they were seasonal and badly paid, were out of work in a country where there is no unemployment compensation. The manager contributed to poverty, so he performed a political action. Secondly, as long as the fruit was being peeled by hand, the little river next to the factory was clean, crystal clear and full of fish. Now it is a stinking, dead sewer. Those poor people not only lost the little money they were earning, they also lost a resource—good protein out of the river. But there was still another loss. As long as the fruit was being peeled by hand, the five factories together produced about 5,000 tons of peel a year to be fed to pigs which also provided a source of food. So we lost jobs, a river and pigs. And who made a profit? Only the industry. When that technocrat made that decision to go for more efficiency, he actually made a political decision. This kind of decision should only be made in a local parliament; the whole population should decide such a question. Perhaps somewhere else in the world it would have been appropriate to do it—somewhere like Stockholm, for example, where they don't have all those poor people—but there they would have also asked for a treatment station to recycle the effluent.

Every technological decision is a political one. But we don't yet have the necessary political critique of technology so that we can analyse each technology according to whether it is good for society as a whole or only for a few powerful people. That does not mean we have to give

165

up technology—quite the contrary—but it does mean we have to go for soft technology, technology conceived in the interests of people. We have to find a way of evolving in that direction.

If we are to escape from our current predicament, we need a completely new economic model, one that abandons the fallacies of technocratic thinking and is based on ecological thinking instead, a model that includes perfect recycling and that uses only that energy we really have—namely solar energy. All the permanently sustainable forms of energy we have on this planet, such as hydro energy, are forms of solar energy. When we introduce energy from outside, whether it be by splitting the atom or by putting panels in space to reflect additional sunlight to this planet, then we are in trouble because we are upsetting the balance and putting too much energy onto the planet.

Above all, we need a new religion—one of reverence for life, like that preached by Albert Schweitzer and St Francis, and like that practised by many of the old non-Christian cultures such as the American Indians, who believed that every aspect of the natural world was important and that they themselves were part of the whole of life. It is a Gaian religion that we need, through which we may learn to see ourselves not as the conquerors of nature but as its stewards. OF SOCIETY

Appendix

The Findhorn Foundation and Finance

Alex Walker

At the conference on 'The New Economic Agenda' at the Findhorn Foundation in 1984, there were many requests for more information about the Foundation's approach to finance and economics. It is in response to these requests that the following chapter by Alex Walker is included in this book. Alex, a former research assistant in the Department of Management Studies at the University of Glasgow, has been working with the finances of the Findhorn Foundation for the last four years, and is a member of the Foundation's Management Committee.

The Findhorn Foundation is an international spiritual community in the north of Scotland committed to deepening humanity's understanding of life and the improvement of human relationships. It welcomes people of all backgrounds and beliefs and offers them an opportunity to discover their true nature as spiritual beings able to make a positive and constructive difference in the world.

Situated near the small fishing village of Findhorn, the Foundation began in 1962 with an experiment in new ways of working with nature. Despite poor soil and adverse conditions, the results achieved in the cultivation of flowers and vegetables offered impressive evidence of the power of working in harmony and cooperation with the nature realms. The garden became a source of deep inspiration to many. As a small community formed, its members were united by a desire to better their relationships with one another, their environment and their sense of higher purpose or divinity. Educational programmes were developed to help them do this, attracting hundreds and then thousands of visitors each year.

Currently, there is a growing recognition of the role of finance and money within the Foundation, and of the community's potential role in bringing about a greater awareness of the spiritual nature of these subjects. Whilst the Foundation's experience has been more in the nature of an experiment than a role model, we hope that an exploration of our financial policies might result in their having a wider relevance.

The Foundation's financial policy to date has been governed by three main principles: manifestation based on faith; the twin concepts of manifestation and stewardship; and the process of cellular evolution. A fourth guiding principle which has been emerging over the past 18 months is that of 'Foundation and Village'. Although these ideas have come to fruition in this order, they are in fact inter-related, the seed of each one being contained within the previous one. All form part of a developing theme of 'right livelihood' and should not be seen or treated separately.

I will examine briefly the nature of these principles and how they have been put into practical effect in the Foundation's work, and then go on to look to the future, concentrating in particular on the economic implications of the fourth guiding principle, Foundation and Village.

Manifestation Based on Faith.

In the pamphlet *Findhorn and Finance*, published by the Foundation in 1973, it is stated: "When one gives up all in perfect trust and willingness to serve God, and lives in harmony with his laws and his will, then all one's needs are perfectly met, often in far greater ways than one might have dreamed."

In a world where the economic problems of the day are so well known and yet so intractable, it may seem difficult to embrace this statement. How can we reconcile it with a knowledge of ecological imbalance, unemployment, the nuclear arms race and Third World debt and poverty? The key lies in the recognition that working with the spiritual or inner nature of economics requires attention to the *potential* of any given situation as well as to its actual or apparent nature. As David Spangler says in *The Laws of Manifestation*, "Manifestation is a process of working with natural principles and laws in order to translate energy from one level of reality to another. It is not the creation of something out of nothing, but rather a process of realising a potential of something that already exists."

Faith and service are key elements in this principle. Faith means much more than hopefulness: it is *knowing* that the substance of God and the abundance of the spiritual realms are more real than the apparent world revealed through our senses. Nor is service to be understood in terms of sacrifice or duty, but rather as a blending of one's self in the opportunity of creative partnership. Faith is the knowing, often transcending the knowledge of the human mind and its logical analysis, and service is the dynamic action of creativity based on that knowing.

In the early days of the community the principle of manifestation based on faith was adhered to by following the inner 'guidance' and intuition of Eileen and Peter Caddy and Dorothy Maclean, the founders, and R. Ogilvie Crombie. Their remarkable success in addressing the practical needs and assessing the potential role of the Findhorn community has been well documented (see, for instance, *The Magic of Findhorn* by Paul Hawken) so perhaps a single example will suffice here.

"It was one manifestation after another," says Eileen Caddy. "Sometimes it took a while after the thought was put out to achieve the physical reality, but often it would happen quite quickly. For instance, we needed a music system for the sanctuary (meditation room), and a regular visitor offered his radiogramme and speakers which he said were too big for his own house. Not only did he bring it up from the north of England for us, but he also brought a carpet for the sanctuary as well, and laid it personally. When I received guidance about something, I knew it would come, and often just the right object or amount of money would be given to us. There was always the question of timing though. When I was told we would be going back to Cluny Hill hotel 'soon', I didn't think we'd have to wait 13 years!"

The economic basis of the community's early activity was small—almost negligible—in comparison with the million pound charity that is the Findhorn Foundation today. Conducted from a handful of caravans and bungalows, it often utilised the unwanted materials cast aside by others—manure for the original garden from a nearby stables, over-ripe vegetables for soup, castaway cement and timber for building materials.

An important aspect of the nascent community's life at this time was its work with the nature kingdoms and the natural cycles of the Earth. These natural rhythms were and are influential on our economic system, and there is an enduring link between the two. Just as nature here has an abundant summer and a more introspective winter, so our own cash flow peaks in the summer and this harvest is required to see us through the quieter days and longer nights later in the year.

When the community grew beyond a few dozen individuals a more sophisticated set of guidelines was required. Much of this philosophical development was articulated by David Spangler, a young lecturer from the USA (the greater portion of the membership was from America at this time), and his thoughts on the 'laws of manifestation' added a more comprehensive framework to the original ideas. He divided the process of working the laws of manifestation into four stages—Right Identification, Right Imagination, Right Attunement and Right Action, and stressed the need to see such actions as proceeding from a sense of wholeness and oneness with all life, rather than from separation, fear and lack.

Stewardship and Manifestation

In tandem with this work, the Trustees of the newly formed Findhorn Trust (later the Findhorn Foundation) began to develop the second theme of stewardship and manifestation. These two concepts have underlain much of the Foundation's growth, and the interplay between them has influenced a great deal of our recent history. Stewardship is our pledge to the kingdoms that surround and nourish us, and essentially commits us to being wise caretakers of that with which we have been entrusted, as well as to covering day-to-day living expenses from our earnings. Manifestation, on the other hand, recognises that any expansion of our work or facilities will need to be supported and financed by other than our own resources alone, and that any such expansion involves clearly identifying the greater need or potential it serves, and then proceeding in the faith that all required to realise that potential will be provided.

The two ideas are closely related. For instance, the community's close attention to good financial housekeeping on our operating account cleared the channels for the Caravan Park Appeal Fund. This appeal, which enabled us to buy the land that had been our home for 21 years, raised over £250,000 in a little over a year. The purchase of the Park as a going concern is, in turn, enabling us to fulfil our promise of good stewardship more fully.

However, this, the finest example of the process to date, came after a long period of learning, experimentation and, indeed, doubt. The two major challenges we faced were the social problems created by a rapidly growing membership and the financial problems ensuing from the policy of borrowing capital to finance expansion. New assets were purchased both to accommodate all who wanted to participate in the by now well-known 'university of light' (as the community began to style itself) and also to house the new activities that were being planned in the fields of the arts, education and business.

The first new asset to be purchased was the Cluny Hill Hydro, an

80-bedroom hotel in the nearby town of Forres. In order to do this £65,000 was borrowed. This was no doubt a sensible move in itself, but it proved to be the first step on a somewhat slippery and treacherous slope. Further new properties followed apace. Drumduan House, also in Forres, was generously donated, Cullerne House and gardens were purchased for £80,000, then Station House in Findhorn village was acquired. The burden of debt grew. Next, the Isle of Erraid on the West coast of Scotland was lent to us by its Dutch owners, and while this did not add to our structural debt, the costs of operating the island and the other properties made it increasingly difficult to run the Foundation on a break-even basis. Work had also begun on the 'Universal Hall', a large theatre and arts complex, and the costs had burgeoned far beyond original expectations. Over £300,000 in materials alone were expended on this project between 1976 and 1983.

In other words, the principle of manifestation based on faith had been modified (if not actually abandoned) by taking on loans rather than waiting on funds to become available without strings attached. This in turn meant that stewardship was becoming increasingly difficult under the burden of loan interest and increased operating costs. In order to grapple with these difficulties the Trustees conceived a new and complementary strategy—that of 'cellular development'.

Cellular Evolution

The background to the development of this process was the growth of the community's membership from 120 in 1973 to over 300 by 1979. As has been well documented in many other cooperative environments, increasing size leads to considerable difficulties in communication. The answer to this challenge in the Foundation was perceived to be a natural organic growth whereby the different functional groups or 'cells' of the community would begin to take greater responsibility for their well-being on both spiritual and practical levels—for their own finances, personnel, maintenance and spiritual life.

The first real experiment undertaken was on Erraid. After an initial few years of losses during which time the Foundation capitalised the Erraid project, it was made clear to the group that further subsidy from the centre could not be contemplated. Within a short period the island became entirely self-supporting and has in fact made handsome surpluses over the last three years or so.

An extension of this theme was the formation of New Findhorn Directions (NFD) Ltd, a limited liability company wholly owned by the

172

Trustees of the Foundation. The impulse behind this development was the desire to provide a holding company so that commercial activities instigated by members could be carried on outside the umbrella of the charitable trust, but within an environment that would protect a new business from the full rigours of the financial climate during its crucial first years. One such company, Weatherwise Solar, a home insulation/solar heating concern, began under the auspices of NFD and has now become completely independent. Findhorn Bay Caravan Park (which runs the commercial caravan site that was purchased along with the land) is the sole division at present, but others are envisaged for the future.

As the philosophy of cellular evolution developed and the community began to overcome its teenage financial difficulties, a fourth ideal emerged, that of Foundation and Village. In this, the purchase of the Caravan Park is a key factor, one which is more significant than just providing us with a means to repay our debt and the space to expand our activities, vital though these benefits are. It is also an important statement about our permanence and our commitment to the development of a sustainable and holistic lifestyle on a long-term basis. There is now a growing feeling that the last 18 months or so represent a transition phase between the stage of *community* and a new stage of *village*, a springboard for a step into a new phase of economic and social organisation.

At this early stage it is not at all clear what the characteristics of this next phase will be. However, various developments are currently emerging which may help to give some indication as to their nature. The most important appear to be financial diversity; financial stability; a building programme; debt reduction, and the creative use of capital.

Financial Diversity
In the context of the Foundation and its spiritual work, the idea of 'community' has come to imply a structure which embraces a group of individuals with common goals and lifestyles, living and working together within a single legal and economic framework. 'Village', however, tends to indicate a greater diversity. Villages have independent—even competing—shops and businesses, more diverse and individualised lifestyles, dwelling places, financial circumstances, and a plethora of legal structures to cover the butcher, the baker and the candlestick-maker. 'Village' may also imply a less transient state of affairs than the idea of a community.

Expressed in this way, the Foundation has found itself between two stools for some time. The lifestyles of Cluny Hill, the Park and Erraid are different as well as physically distant from one another. The Cluny baker and the Erraid candlestick-maker may have similar spiritual goals and aspirations, but their daily experience of community differs radically. However, until recently almost all the ventures spawned by the community have been under one legal heading—the Foundation as charitable trust. Furthermore, all staff members have received the same 'wage' (an allowance currently set at £10 a week); and mobility between, say, the garden and the personnel department has been both swift and easy to accomplish.

Nonetheless, the last few years have seen a flourishing diversity of new concerns which are associated with, but not part of, the Foundation itself. These include Weatherwise Solar and Findhorn Bay Caravan Park, plus Newbold House (an independent charity in its own right situated in Forres and running similar programmes to our own) and Minton House healing centre, as well as a variety of independent and semi-independent individual members. In addition, more attention is now being given to a number of activities that previously have had only a peripheral or occasional profile in the community's work. These include various healing techniques, sacred dance and a primary school. Others for the future may be work with youth, a recording studio, a research faculty and a building school.

Although this trend towards greater diversity is a logical step along the route of cellular growth, it does not mean that the Foundation will mitotically divide into small independent units, and that the village structure will completely replace the present community. Few members would wish to see the Community Centre become a restaurant, Cluny Hill a separate college or the studios turned into private businesses. But it does seem likely that an important aspect of village life will be the growing number of individuals who are involved in the wider work of the community, but who are not full-time members of the Foundation. If this is the case, no doubt much of the challenge of future years will be concerned with the integration of this change in a balanced way.

Indeed, it is likely that the Foundation will remain as the central core, both the entry point for new energies/individuals/ideas/emergent businesses, and the keeper of the spiritual message that forms the seedbed for the surrounding activities of a more independent nature. Although no comparison can be fully adequate, perhaps the structure will look a little like that of a small university town, with the Foundation still the key point, but no longer the totality.

Financial Stability
A key characteristic of the years 1979-82 was our communal inability to make ends meet on a regular basis. The rapid expansion of the previous four years had left us with high operating costs and a burden of loan interest which was increasingly difficult to carry. Between 1979-82 we made no reduction in our overall debt—in fact, our indebtedness increased from £307,000 to £350,000—while our net operating deficit for this time was around £30,000. These years saw a period of retrenchment as we struggled to iron out our financial and personnel difficulties: some assets were sold, 'non-essential' activities declined, especially the Arts, and gradually efficiency and accountability increased. The very challenge of tackling these problems helped unite the community and led to the successful Caravan Park appeal. In 1983 and 1984 we made a net surplus of close to £60,000, without including the Caravan Park appeal or any of the income from operating the Caravan Park as a business.

Although the future will no doubt bring its challenges, we seem to have moved out of a period of crisis management into one of increasing prosperity and options, where there is more to consider than the imperatives of economic survival. One of these subjects worthy of attention is the building programme.

Building Programme
In becoming the owner of the Caravan Park, the Foundation has made a powerful statement about its permanence, and our next step here is likely to be the replacement of the present mobile homes and temporary structures with more durable buildings. However, the village context implies first and foremost a *way* of life, and the physical structures we create will reflect rather than impose a lifestyle. Whilst the two will obviously grow in tandem and form intertwined parts of a co-creative process, it would be more accurate to suggest that the construction programme will be housing the village rather than building it.

Our two most pressing needs are improving and expanding our accommodation, and replacing or expanding the Community Centre. Housing for our growing membership is insufficient for current needs, while many of the caravans are now coming to the end of their useful life. Accommodation for guests is also stretched to its limits for many weeks of the year. If we are to expand our membership and educational programmes at all, a programme of new building is essential.

The Community Centre has been a faithful servant for many years, but it too is now beginning to show the stress and strain of this service. During the busiest weeks of the year it is filled to—and beyond—capacity. If our numbers are to increase and if the Universal Hall is to be used to its full capacity, the Community Centre must be substantially renovated and enlarged. Clearly both these major new developments will require financing as well as envisioning, and financing that is currently beyond the scope of our own operating resources. As always, we move in faith.

Debt Reduction

The growth of the Foundation's indebtedness occurred during two brief but explosive periods. The first was during the phase of expansion when structural debt first emerged and quickly rose to over £300,000, and the second was in 1983 when the completion of the Hall and the purchase of the Caravan Park sent the debt soaring again to just short of £500,000. Since then the Caravan Park loan has been entirely eliminated and debt is is now once more at the £300-350,000 mark.

One of the prime financial reasons for wishing to purchase the Park was to have a means of paying off the balance of our outstanding debts, for although the rise in debt had been accompanied by a concomitant rise in our fixed assets (Cluny Hill, Cullerne, Station House, the Universal Hall), a number of difficulties began to emerge in the late 1970s. High interest rates made the servicing of this debt a considerable burden. The growth of the community had slowed and even been arrested, making repayment of the capital an increasingly unrealistic task. Another important influence has been a growing feeling that loan financing may no longer be appropriate for the community. It is not that borrowing money is thought to be wrong *per se*: rather that its role is perhaps more useful in business where return on capital is a major motivation.

Spiritual communities have of course to pay some homage to mammon if they are to survive and have relevance in the modern world, but the order of priorities is nevertheless different from that of a limited company. It is now widely believed that we can function effectively and well without the encumbrance of a debt. We therefore intend to place £50,000 per year from the profit of the Caravan Park business towards debt reduction. This, with a little help from other sources, should entirely eliminate the debt by the end of the 80s.

The debt itself has come in a variety of guises, and today the three most important are the bank overdraft (£100,000); loans from private individuals on the Cullerne property (£46,000); and general private loans (£190,000). At this time it is not yet clear which debt we will attempt to eliminate first, as the constantly changing financial circumstances of our personal and corporate lenders make prophecy a risky business.

Creative Use of Capital

However, a paradox emerges. Whilst the motivations of those lending money to the Foundation have no doubt been as varied as the individuals concerned, an important factor has certainly been the desire to invest money in a concern they personally supported, as opposed to placing their assets in morally neutral profit maximising ventures.

It is hoped that the Foundation's drive to reduce its debts will not remove this particular option. As more and more people begin to question the ethics of the businesses their money is tied up in, a strong movement for 'socially responsible investing' has emerged. Our role in this field is still nascent, but we hope to have concrete proposals soon.

Currently there is over £300,000 of private capital in the community's hands. This includes the members' savings club, now standing at over £100,000. Other than direct investment in the Foundation's work, which will take less and less of this sum as the overall debt is reduced, there are two other possibilities available.

1) Investment in village activities/businesses outside the Foundation.

2) Making use of the Foundation's stock-broking facilities to reinvest monies in other socially responsible ways. We are registered clients of Phillips and Drew of the London Exchange, and we are exploring methods of extending this facility to members and friends of the community.

In many ways we are in a similar position to the one we faced just after the beginning of the last period of expansion in 1975. We have borrowed a substantial sum of money to purchase assets with considerable financial potential; now we are anticipating the return which will clear those debts. That previous period was in many ways highly successful, but it left a residue of difficulties which took several years to clear up. If we have learnt the lessons of that time well, we can look forward to the emerging village of abundance.

Further Reading

Rudolf Bahro, **From Red to Green**, Verso, London, 1984

Edward de Bono, **Atlas of Management Thinking**, Penguin, Harmondsworth, 1983.

David Bohm, **Wholeness and the Implicate Order**, Ark Paperbacks, London, 1983.

Brandt Commission, **North-South: A Programme for Survival**, Pan Books, London and Sydney, 1980. **Common Crisis**, Pan Books, 1983.

The Briarpatch Book, New Glide/Reed, San Francisco/Los Angeles, 1978.

Lester Brown, **Building a Sustainable Society**, Norton, New York, 1983.

William Clark, **Cataclysm: The North-South Conflict of 1987**, Sidgwick & Jackson.

Herman Daly (ed), **Toward a Steady-State Economy**, Freeman, San Francisco, 1973.

Erik Dammann, **The Future in our Hands**, Pergamon Press, Oxford, 1979.

Guy Dauncey, **The Unemployment Handbook**, National Extension College, Cambridge, 1982. **Nice Work if You can Get It**, National Extension College, 1983.

Erik Eckholm, **Down to Earth**, Pluto Press, London, 1982.

Duane Elgin, **Voluntary Simplicity**, Morrow, New York, 1981.

George Gilder, **Wealth and Poverty**, Basic Books, New York, 1981.

Charles Handy, **The Future of Work**, Blackwell, Oxford and New York, 1984.

Paul Hawken, **The Next Economy**, Holt, Rinehart and Winston, New York, 1983; Angus and Robertson, London, 1984.

Paul Hawken, James Ogilvy and Peter Schwartz, **Seven Tomorrows: Toward a Voluntary History**, Bantam Books, New York, 1982.

Hazel Henderson, **Creating Alternative Futures: The End of Economics**, Berkeley Windover, New York, 1978. **The Politics of the Solar Age**, Anchor/Doubleday, New York, 1981.

Clive Jenkins and Barrie Sherman, **The Collapse of Work**, Methuen.

Warren Johnson, **Muddling Toward Frugality: A Blueprint for Survival in the 1980s**, Sierra Club Books, San Francisco, 1978.

Barry Jones, **Sleepers Wake! Technology and the Future of Work,** Wheatsheaf Books, Brighton, 1982.

Bill Jordan, **Automatic Poverty,** Routledge and Kegan Paul, London, 1981.

Francis Kinsman, **The New Agenda,** Spencer Stuart Management Consultants, 1983.

Phil Laut, **Money is My Friend,** Trinity, California, 1978.

Jim Lovelock, **Gaia: A New Look at Life on Earth,** Oxford University Press, Oxford, 1979.

Manfred Max-Neef, **From the Outside Looking In: Experiences in Barefoot Economics,** Dag Hammarskjold Foundation, 1982.

Giles Merritt, **World out of Work,** Collins, 1982.

James Ogilvy, **Many Dimensional Man: Decentralising Self, Society and the Sacred,** Oxford University Press, New York, 1977.

Thomas Peters and Robert Waterman, **In Search of Excellence,** Harper & Row, New York, 1982.

Michael Phillips, **The Seven Laws of Money,** World Wheel, California and Random House, New York, 1974.

Jonathon Porritt, **Seeing Green: The Politics of Ecology Explained,** Blackwell, Oxford and New York, 1984.

James Robertson, **The Sane Alternative,** published privately, 1983.

E.F. Schumacher, **Small is Beautiful; A Guide for the Perplexed; and Good Work.** Abacus, London.

Graeme Shankland, **A Guide to the Informal Economy,** Report for 'Work and Society', London, 1984.

Tony Stonier, **The Wealth of Information: A Profile of the Post-Industrial Society,** Methuen, London, 1983.

Papers from TOES (The Other Economic Summit), London, 1984.

Lestor Thurow, **The Zero-Sum Society: Distribution and Possibilities for Economic Change,** Basic Books, New York, 1980.

Tony Watts, **Education, Unemployment and the Future of Work,** Open University, Milton Keynes, 1983.

John Wilson, **After Affluence: Economics to Meet Human Needs,** Harper & Row, New York, 1980.